MAKING HISTORY

Brian Friel was born in Omagh, Co. Tyrone, in 1929. His plays include *Translations*, *Philadelphia, Here I Come!*, *The Loves of Cass McGuire*, *Lovers*, *Freedom of the City*, *Volunteers*, *Living Quarters*, *Faith Healer*, *Dancing at Lughnasa* and *The Communication Cord*. In 1980 he founded the touring theatre company, Field Day, with Stephen Rea.

Michael Etherton, in *Contemporary Irish Dramatists* (Macmillan), writes:

> Brian Friel is one of the most accomplished playwrights working in English today. His work is developed around a central poetic vision which has found, and enhanced, a language of theatre to communicate difficult ideas. This language of drama works through wider poetic sensibilities we actually share with the playwright but which we have lost sight of. Brian Friel sharpens our perceptions and makes us able to understand our human condition and the deepening ironies and contradictions of our age. This is his poetic vision.

by the same author

THE ENEMY WITHIN
PHILADELPHIA, HERE I COME!
THE LOVES OF CASS MAGUIRE
LOVERS
VOLUNTEERS
LIVING QUARTERS
THE FREEDOM OF THE CITY
THREE SISTERS (Chekhov)
ARISTOCRATS
THE COMMUNICATION CORD
MAKING HISTORY
FATHERS AND SONS (after Turgenev)
THE LONDON VERTIGO (after Charles Macklin)
DANCING AT LUGHNASA
WONDERFUL TENNESSEE
MOLLY SWEENEY
GIVE ME YOUR ANSWER, DO
TRANSLATIONS
FAITH HEALER
THREE PLAYS AFTER
PERFORMANCES
THE HOME PLACE
UNCLE VANYA (Chekhov)

BRIAN FRIEL: PLAYS ONE
(*Philadelphia, Here I Come!, The Freedom of the City,
Living Quarters, Aristocrats, Faith Healer, Translations*)

BRIAN FRIEL: PLAYS TWO
(*Dancing at Lughnasa, Fathers and Sons, Making History,
Wonderful Tennessee, Molly Sweeney*)

also available

FABER CRITICAL GUIDE: BRIAN FRIEL
(*Philadelphia, Here I Come!, Translations,
Making History, Dancing at Lughnasa*)

BRIAN FRIEL

Making History

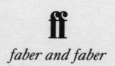

faber and faber

First published in 1989
by Faber and Faber Limited
3 Queen Square London WC1N 3AU

Photoset by Parker Typesetting Service Leicester
Printed and bound in Great Britain by
Mackays of Chatham PLC, Chatham, Kent
All rights reserved

British Library Cataloguing in Publication Data
is available

ISBN 0-571-15477-8

16 18 20 19 17

For
Basil and Helen

CHARACTERS

HUGH O'NEILL	Earl of Tyrone
HARRY HOVEDEN	O'Neill's private secretary
HUGH O'DONNELL	Earl of Tyrconnell
PETER LOMBARD	Titular Bishop of Armagh and Primate of All Ireland
MABEL	Countess. O'Neill's wife
MARY BAGENAL	Mabel's sister

ACT 1

Before Kinsale

Scene 1   O'Neill's house in Dungannon
Scene 2   The same

ACT 2

After Kinsale

Scene 1   The Sperrin mountains
Scene 2   Penitenzieri Palace, Rome

Making History was first performed by Field Day Theatre Company in the Guildhall, Derry, on 20 September 1988. The cast was as follows:

HUGH O'NEILL	Stephen Rea
HARRY HOVEDEN	Niall O'Brien
ARCHBISHOP LOMBARD	Niall Toibin
HUGH O'DONNELL	Peter Gowan
MABEL (BAGENAL) O'NEILL	Clare Holman
MARY BAGENAL	Emma Dewhurst
Director	Simon Curtis
Set designer	Julian McGowan
Lighting designer	Rory Dempster

ACT I

SCENE I

*A large living room in O'Neill's home in Dungannon, County Tyrone,
Ireland. Late August in 1591. The room is spacious and scantily
furnished: a large, refectory-type table; some chairs and stools; a
sideboard. No attempt at decoration.*
O'NEILL *moves around this comfortless room quickly and
energetically, inexpertly cutting the stems off flowers, thrusting the
flowers into various vases and then adding water. He is not listening to*
HARRY HOVEDEN *who consults and reads from various papers on the
table.*

O'NEILL *is forty-one. A private, sharp-minded man at this moment
uncharacteristically outgoing and talkative. He always speaks in an
upper-class English accent except on those occasions specifically
scripted.* HARRY HOVEDEN, *his personal secretary, is about the same
age as* O'NEILL. O'NEILL *describes him as a man 'who has a
comforting and a soothing effect'.*

HARRY: That takes care of Friday. Saturday you're free all day –
so far. Then on Sunday – that'll be the fourteenth –
O'Hagan's place at Tullyhogue. A big christening party. The
invitation came the day you left. I've said you'll be there. All
right?
(*Pause.*)
It's young Brian's first child – you were at his wedding last
year. It'll be a good day.
(*Pause.*)
Hugh?
O'NEILL: Yes?
HARRY: O'Hagan's – where you were fostered.
O'NEILL: Tell me the name of these again.
HARRY: Broom.
O'NEILL: Broom. That's it.
HARRY: The Latin name is *genista*. Virgil mentions it somewhere.
O'NEILL: Does he really?
HARRY: Actually that *genista* comes from Spain.

I

(O'NEILL *looks at the flowers in amazement.*)

O'NEILL: Good Lord – does it? Spanish broom – magnificent name, isn't it?

HARRY: Give them plenty of water.

O'NEILL: Magnificent colour, isn't it?

HARRY: A letter from the Lord Deputy –

O'NEILL: They really transform the room. Splendid idea of yours, Harry. Thank you.

(O'NEILL *silently mouths the word* Genista *again and then continues distributing the flowers.*)

HARRY: A letter from the Lord Deputy 'vigorously urging you to have your eldest son attend the newly established College of the Holy and Undivided Trinity in Dublin founded by the Most Serene Queen Elizabeth'. That 'vigorously urging' sounds ominous, doesn't it?

O'NEILL: Sorry?

HARRY: Sir William Fitzwilliam wants you to send young Hugh to the new Trinity College. I'm told he's trying to get all the big Gaelic families to send their children there. He would like an early response.

O'NEILL: This jacket – what do you think, Harry? It's not a bit . . . excessive, is it?

HARRY: Excessive?

O'NEILL: You know . . . a little too – too strident?

HARRY: Strident?

O'NEILL: All right, damn it, too bloody young?

HARRY: (*Looking at his papers*) It's very becoming, Hugh.

O'NEILL: Do you think so? Maybe I should have got it in maroon.

(*He goes off to get more flowers.*)

HARRY: A reminder that the Annual Festival of Harpers takes place next month in Roscommon. They've changed the venue to Roosky. You're Patron of the Festival and they would be very honoured if you would open the event with a short –

(*He now sees that he is alone. He looks through his papers. Pause.* O'NEILL *enters again with an armful of flowers.*)

O'NEILL: Genista.

HARRY: Yes.

O'NEILL: Spanish broom.

HARRY: Really?

O'NEILL: They need plenty of water.

HARRY: A bit of trouble. O'Kane of Limavady says he can't
pay his tribute until the harvest is saved but in the
meantime he's sending ten firkins of butter and twenty
casks of beer. As usual he's lying. It might be an idea to
billet fifty extra gallowglass on him for the next quarter.
That'll keep him in line. Sir Garret Moore invites you
down to Mellifont Abbey for a few days' fishing on the
Boyne. He says it's the best salmon season he's ever had.
The Lord Chancellor'll be there. And Sir Robert
Gardener. You knew him when you were in England,
didn't you?

O'NEILL: Who's that?

HARRY: Sir Robert Gardener, the Lord Chief Justice.

O'NEILL: Oh, that was twenty-five years ago. Haven't seen him
since.

HARRY: Might be worth renewing that friendship now.

O'NEILL: (*Tyrone accent*) Just to show him I haven't reverted
completely to type — would that be it?

HARRY: For political reasons.

O'NEILL: We'll see. Have the musicians arrived?

HARRY: Yes.

O'NEILL: And the rhymers and the acrobats?

HARRY: I've told you — everything's ready.

O'NEILL: And you're sure nobody has heard a whisper?

HARRY: I've said you were in Dublin at a meeting of the
Council. Everything's in hand.

O'NEILL: Good.

(O'NEILL *continues with his flowers.*)

HARRY: And more trouble: the Devlins and the Quinns are at
each other's throats again. The Quinns raided the Devlins'
land three times last week; killed five women and two
children; stole cattle and horses and burned every hayfield
in sight. The Devlins remind you — once more they say —
that they have the right to expect protection from their
chieftain and that if Hugh O'Neill cannot offer them safety

3

and justice under the Brehon Law, they'll have to look for protection under the new English Law. And they will, too.

O'NEILL: I know what I'll do, Harry.

HARRY: That's a squabble needs to be sorted out quickly.

O'NEILL: I'll make the room upstairs into our bedroom! And I'll shift that consignment of Spanish saddles down to the back room. They should be closer to the stables anyway. The room upstairs faces south and there's a good view down to the river. Yes – that's a good decision. Don't you agree?

HARRY: Why not?

O'NEILL: Excellent.

(O'NEILL *returns to his flowers*.)

HARRY: Bad news from London. Young Essex's been arrested and thrown in the Tower.

(O'NEILL *stops working*.)

O'NEILL: What for?

HARRY: There's a list of charges. One of them is treason.

O'NEILL: Damn it.

HARRY: 'For conferring secretly with the basest and vilest traitor that ever lived, Hugh O'Neill, in a manner most disloyal to Her Majesty, Queen Elizabeth.'

O'NEILL: Damn it.

HARRY: He was fond of you.

O'NEILL: I was fond of him – despite everything.

HARRY: I know.

O'NEILL: Crazy man.

(*Short pause*.)

HARRY: What else is there? Hugh O'Donnell and Peter Lombard want to see you.

O'NEILL: All right. Some day next week.

HARRY: They're here, Hugh.

O'NEILL: Now?!

HARRY: Waiting outside. Mind elsewhere

O'NEILL: Oh, come on, Harry! I'm scarcely in the door –

HARRY: O'Donnell knows you're home. And the Archbishop's been waiting here four days for you. And he has done an enormous amount of work. (*Points to a large pile of papers*.) That's only half of his file.

4

O'NEILL: Oh, my God. All right – I'll give them ten minutes and that's all.

HARRY: Did you know that he's begun writing a book on you?

O'NEILL: (*Suddenly alert*) Lombard?

HARRY: So he told me.

O'NEILL: We have our own annalist.

HARRY: He knows that.

O'NEILL: What sort of book?

HARRY: He said something about a history – I don't know – *The Life and Times of Hugh O'Neill*, I imagine.

O'NEILL: He might have told me about that.

HARRY: He spent all Tuesday checking dates with me.

O'NEILL: I don't think I like this idea at all.

HARRY: Maybe I got it all wrong. Ask him yourself. And this (*letter*) – you'll want to read this yourself. It arrived a few hours ago.

O'NEILL: What's that?

HARRY: From Newry.
(*He reaches the letter towards* O'NEILL. O'NEILL *stretches out to take it – and then withdraws his hand.*)

O'NEILL: Bagenal?

HARRY: Bagenal.

O'NEILL: Her father or her brother?

HARRY: Brother.

O'NEILL: Give me that! No, no, read it to me.

HARRY: 'From Sir Henry Bagenal, Queen's Marshal, Newry, to Sir Hugh O'Neill, Earl of Tyrone, Dungannon – '
(O'NEILL *clicks his fingers impatiently.*)
(*Reluctantly*) It's a – it's just a catalogue of accusation and personal abuse. Your first marriage was never properly dissolved. So your second marriage was ambiguous. And of course this third.

O'NEILL: Bastard.

HARRY: He's threatening to bring a charge of abduction against you.

O'NEILL: What's he talking about?

HARRY: Because she's under twenty-one.

O'NEILL: 'Abduction'!

5

HARRY: He's threatening to come and take her back by force.

O'NEILL: She's not exactly Helen of Troy, for Christ's sake! (*He regrets that instantly.*) And what's that?

HARRY: We got our hands on a copy of a letter he's written to the Queen: 'I am deeply humiliated and ashamed that my blood, which my father and I have often shed in repressing this rebellious race, should now be mingled with so traitorous a stock.'

O'NEILL: 'My blood'! Staffordshire mongrel!

HARRY: He's going to be troublesome, Hugh.

O'NEILL: No wonder our poets call them Upstarts. That's all he is – a bloody Upstart! Ignore him. He'll bluster for a few days. I'm going to see about that bedroom.

(*As he is about to exit,* O'DONNELL *and* LOMBARD *enter.*)

O'DONNELL *is a very young man in his early twenties. He is impulsive, enthusiastic and generous. He has a deep affection for* O'NEILL. ARCHBISHOP LOMBARD *is a contemporary of* O'NEILL. *By profession he is a church diplomat and his manner is careful and exact. But he is also a man of humour and perception and by no means diminished by his profession. He now carries a large candelabra and an elegant birdcage.*

O'DONNELL: I knew I heard the voice!

O'NEILL: Young O'Donnell!

O'DONNELL: How are you, man?

O'NEILL: Good to see you, Hugh. You're welcome.

O'DONNELL: Good to see you, too.

(*They embrace with great affection.*)

I haven't seen you since the horse-swimming at Lough Owel, the day you rode the – ! (*He breaks off.*) Jesus, lads, what about that – eh? Is that not a sight for sore eyes!

O'NEILL: Do you like it?

O'DONNELL: I bet you that's a London job – eh?

O'NEILL: Of course.

O'DONNELL: And the smell of perfume off him!

O'NEILL: Peter.

LOMBARD: How are you, Hugh?

6

religion for politics

O'NEILL: Welcome back to Dungannon.

LOMBARD: Thank you.

womaniser

O'DONNELL: My poor sister's not seven months dead and I bet you the bugger's on the prowl again! (*To* HARRY) Am I right? (HARRY *spreads his hands.*)

LOMBARD: Gifts for you, Hugh. From the Pope. *straight to bus.*

O'NEILL: What's all this?

LOMBARD: A silver birdcage and a gold and silver candelabra.

O'DONNELL: Look at that for craftsmanship.

O'NEILL: Lovely. Indeed. Beautiful.

O'DONNELL: He sent me a present, too. Guess what I got – a papal blessing! *chu duce*

LOMBARD: (*To* O'NEILL) With his warmest good wishes.

O'NEILL: I'm not being paid off, am I?

LOMBARD: He's solidly behind you in principle.

O'NEILL: He always is. But no money?

LOMBARD: These things take time, Hugh. I've a letter from him for you too.

O'NEILL: (*Aside to* HARRY) See about that room now. (*To* LOMBARD) So you're just back from Rome?

LOMBARD: Home a week last Sunday. Came via Spain. I've a lot to report.

O'NEILL: Good. Will you sit here, Peter?
(HARRY *exits.* O'DONNELL *goes to the sideboard where there are bottles, wine and glasses.*)

LOMBARD: (*Sits*) Thank you.

O'DONNELL: Can we help ourselves, Hugh?

O'NEILL: Of course. Sorry. Peter? *no distractions*

LOMBARD: Not for me, thanks. I have copies here for everybody.

O'DONNELL: Do you know that the floor in the hall out there is going to cave in with dry rot?

LOMBARD: This is all the recent correspondence with Spain – our case to Philip II and his responses, including his last reply which you haven't seen yet.

O'DONNELL: We had dry rot in the house at Ballyshannon and my mother had to tear out every piece of timber in the place.

LOMBARD: And this is a résumé of my *Commentarius* – a thesis I'm doing on the Irish situation. Briefly my case is this.

Because of her mismanagement England has forfeited her right to domination over this country. The Irish chieftains have been forced to take up arms in defence of their religion. And because of your birth, education and personal attributes, you are the natural leader of that revolt. I'll go into it in detail later on.

O'DONNELL: Do you know what my mother did? She got oak off those Armada wrecks lying about the coast and replaced every floor and window in the house. It's a terrific job. You could gallop a horse across those floors now. You should do the same here, Hugh.

light hearted

O'NEILL: And I hear you're writing our history, Peter?

LOMBARD: Ah. Harry has been talking.

O'NEILL: Have you begun?

LOMBARD: No, no; only checking some events and dates.

O'NEILL: And when your checking is done?

LOMBARD: Then I suppose I'll try to arrange the material into a shape – eventually.

O'NEILL: And interpret what you've gathered?

LOMBARD: Not interpret, Hugh. Just describe.

O'NEILL: Without comment?

LOMBARD: I'll just try to tell the story of what I saw and took part in as accurately as I can.

O'NEILL: But you'll tell the truth?

LOMBARD: I'm no historian, Hugh. I'm not even sure I know what the historian's function is – not to talk of his method.

O'NEILL: But you'll tell the truth?

LOMBARD: If you're asking me will my story be as accurate as possible – of course it will. But are truth and falsity the proper criteria? I don't know. Maybe when the time comes my first responsibility will be to tell the best possible narrative. Isn't that what history is, a kind of story-telling?

O'NEILL: Is it?

LOMBARD: Imposing a pattern on events that were mostly casual and haphazard and shaping them into a narrative that is logical and interesting. Oh, yes, I think so.

O'NEILL: And where does the truth come into all this?

LOMBARD: I'm not sure that 'truth' is a primary ingredient – is

8

that a shocking thing to say? Maybe when the time comes, imagination will be as important as information. But one thing I will promise you: nothing will be put down on paper for years and years. History has to be made – before it's remade.

(HARRY *returns*.)

HARRY: That's being looked after.

O'NEILL: Good. Now, let's make this short and brisk, shall we? What's on the agenda?

HARRY: Hugh has got information that the English are planning new fortifications along the –

O'DONNELL: Do you know what the hoors are at? They're going to build a line of forts right across the country from Dundalk over to Sligo. That'll cut us off from the south. (*He illustrates this by tearing a sheet of paper in two*.) The second stage is to build a huge fort at Derry so that you and I will be cut off from each other. (*He illustrates this by cutting the half-page into quarters*.) Then, when Donegal and Tyrone are isolated, then they plan to move in against each of us.

HARRY: And the Archbishop has news about help from Spain.

LOMBARD: I have letters from both the King and –

O'DONNELL: But their first move is to strengthen the forts they already have: Bagenal's place at Newry; Armagh; and the Blackwater.

LOMBARD: (*As he passes papers around*) I've spent a lot of time in Madrid recently, Hugh, and I can tell you that Europe is looking more and more to us as the ideal springboard for the Counter-Reformation.

O'DONNELL: And another thing I want to talk about: the shit O'Doherty up in Inishowen. Do you know what the wee get's at, Hugh? Nipping down as far as Killybegs, stealing our sheep and shipping them off to France! Running a bloody big export business – with my sheep!

LOMBARD: The initial shock of the Reformation is over. Catholic Europe is now gathering itself together for a Counter-Reformation. And the feeling is that culturally, geographically and with some military assistance we could be the spearhead of that counter-attack.

O'DONNELL: Now I can go in today and snatch the bastard and chop his head off. But if I do that all Inishowen's up in arms and already I have O'Rourke of West Breffny threatening to quarter me.

(O'DONNELL *now joins the others at the table*.)

Did you hear what we did to O'Rourke last week? Jesus, you'll love this, Hugh. We got word that he was away down in Clare at a funeral. So we slipped down to Lough Allen and took away every horse and foal he owns! Six hundred prime animals! Jesus, he's going mad! Because he can't come after us! Because he has no transport! Good one, Hugh – eh?

HARRY: Let's begin with the Archbishop, shall we?

O'DONNELL: You'll help me against the shit O'Doherty, won't you? Because if I do nothing, the bugger'll think he has me bet.

HARRY: You sit there, Hugh.

O'DONNELL: Damn it, maybe I could poison him! The very job! Send him a peace offering – a cask of Bordeaux Special!

LOMBARD: Has everybody got a copy?   modem

O'DONNELL: Or better still you (O'NEILL) send him the Bordeaux. He'd never suspect you. I got a jar of this deadly stuff from Genoa last week – just one drop in your glass and – plunk!

HARRY: Go ahead, Peter.

LOMBARD: Thank you. Three months –

O'DONNELL: All the same that jacket takes years off him.

LOMBARD: If I may, Hugh (O'DONNELL) –

O'DONNELL: You would never think he was forty-one, would you? Almost forty-two. (*Offering* LOMBARD *the floor*) Peter.

LOMBARD: Three months ago you (O'NEILL) wrote again to Philip asking for Spanish arms and money. You have a copy – dated May 14 last.

O'DONNELL: I have no copy.

(HARRY *points to a paper in front of* O'DONNELL.)

Ah. Sorry.

LOMBARD: The final sentence reads: 'With such aid we hope to restore the faith of the Church and to secure you a kingdom.'

O'DONNELL: I never agreed with that stuff about offering him a kingdom.

LOMBARD: I have brought his reply back – the document dated
August 3. 'I have been informed you are defending the
Catholic cause against the English. That this is acceptable to
God is proved by the signal victories you have gained –'

O'DONNELL: Not against the shit O'Doherty.

LOMBARD: 'I hope you will continue to prosper and you need not
doubt but I will render you any assistance you may require.'
Now after all these years I think I have a very good idea how
the Spanish court thinks. They have a natural sympathy and
understanding of us because we share the one true faith. And
they genuinely abhor England's attempt to impose the new
heretical religion on us. But don't assume that that sympathy
is unqualified – because it is not. Their interest in us is
practical and political. I have had a series of meetings with
the Duke of Lerma –

O'DONNELL: Whoever he is.

LOMBARD: He determines their foreign policy. And every time he
says the same thing to me. Spain will help you only if you are
useful to us. And when I look at you what do I see? A small
island located strategically to the west of our enemy,
England. A tiny portion of that island, the area around
Dublin, under English rule. A few New English families
living in isolation round the country. But by far the greater
portion of your island is a Gaelic domain, ruled by Gaelic
chieftains. And how do they behave? Constantly at war –
occasionally with the English – but always, always among
themselves. And how can fragmented and warring tribes be
any use to us?

O'DONNELL: Constantly at war? Jesus, I haven't an enemy in the
world!

LOMBARD: But what Lerma is really saying is that if we can forge
ourselves into a cohesive unit, then, then we can go back to
him and say: we are not fragmented; we are not warring; we
are a united people; now help us. Now to return to my
Commentarius – it's the document with the blue cover. The
full title is *De Regno Hiberniae Sanctorum Insula
Commentarius* –

O'DONNELL: I have no –

(HARRY *points to the document in front of him.*)
Ah, sorry.

LOMBARD: My thesis is this. If we are to understand the Irish situation fully we must go back more than four hundred years – to that famous October 17 when Henry II of England landed here. He had in his hand a copy of Pope Adrian the Fourth's Bull, *Laudabiliter*, making him *Dominus Hiberniae* –

O'DONNELL: Whatever that means.

LOMBARD: King of Ireland. And that Bull had two consequences –

O'NEILL: I got married last night.

(*There is a long, shocked silence.*)

O'DONNELL: What?

O'NEILL: I got married last night.

O'DONNELL: You're a liar! (*To* HARRY) He's a liar! (*To* O'NEILL) You bugger, you never did!

O'NEILL: Yes.

O'DONNELL: God Almighty! (*To* HARRY) You said he was in Dublin at a meeting of the Council.

HARRY: He was in Dublin.

O'DONNELL: Jesus God Almighty! The bloody jacket – didn't I tell you the tail was high!

LOMBARD: You kept that very quiet, Hugh.

O'DONNELL: Who to, you bugger, you? I have it! – the big redhead you had here all last month – that Scotch woman – Annie McDonald!

O'NEILL: No.

LOMBARD: Congratulations.

O'NEILL: Thank you.

O'DONNELL: I've got it! – Brian McSwiney's daughter – the Fanad Whippet – what's her real name? – Cecelia! Jesus, not Cecelia!

(O'NEILL *shakes his head.*)

Who then? Come on, man! Tell us!

LOMBARD: Did you say last night?

O'NEILL: In fact at two o'clock this morning. We eloped . . .

O'DONNELL: 'We el——'! Sweet Jesus God Almighty! We eloped! (*He drums the table in his excitement.*) Lay me down

and bury me decent! The hoor eloped! Yipeeeeee! (*Embraces*
O'NEILL.) Terrific, man! Congratulations!

LOMBARD: Who's the new Countess, Hugh?

O'DONNELL: Jesus, I hope I have the same appetite for it when
I'm your age!

O'NEILL: Neither of you knows her. She's from Newry.

O'DONNELL: Magennis! Siobhan Magennis!

O'NEILL: No. She's –

O'DONNELL: The other sister then – the one with the teeth –
Maeve!

O'NEILL: I met her first only a few months ago. On her twentieth
birthday.

O'DONNELL: She's only – ?!

O'NEILL: Her name is Mabel.

O'DONNELL: (*Very grand*) Mabel.

O'NEILL: She's one of the New English. Her grandfather came
over here from Newcastle-under-Lyme in Staffordshire. He
was given the Cistercian monastery and lands around Newry
and Carlingford – that's what brought them over.
(*Pause.*)

O'DONNELL: Come on, Hugh. Quit the aul fooling. Tell us her
real –

O'NEILL: She is Mabel Bagenal. She is the daughter of the retired
Queen's Marshal. She is the sister of Sir Henry Bagenal, the
present Queen's Marshal.
(*Silence.*) contrast - OD v talkative

HARRY: Anybody for more wine? soothsthings
(*Silence.*)

LOMBARD: Where did you get married?

O'NEILL: The Bishop of Meath married us in Drumcondra – on
the outskirts of Dublin.

LOMBARD: Which Bishop of Meath?

O'NEILL: Tom Jones, the Protestant Bishop. Mabel is a
Protestant.

O'DONNELL: Hold on, Hugh – wait now – wait – wait. You can't
marry into the Upstarts! And a sister of the Butcher Bagenal!
Jesus, man –

O'NEILL: I'm going to ask her to come and meet you.

O'DONNELL: Keep her for a month, Hugh – like that McDonald
woman – that's the very job – keep her for a month and then
kick her out. Amn't I right, Harry? (*To* O'NEILL) She won't

Prejudice

mind, Hugh, honest to God. That's what she'll expect.
Those New English are all half tramps. Give her some
clothes and a few shillings and kick her back home to
Staffordshire.

contrast later

O'NEILL: Her home is Newry.

O'DONNELL: Wherever she's from. (*To* HARRY) That's all she'll
expect. I'm telling you.

O'NEILL: I'm going to ask her to join us.

O'DONNELL: Amn't I right, Peter? *1st thought*

LOMBARD: We have all got to assess the religious and political
implications of this association, Hugh.

O'NEILL: Marriage, Archbishop.

LOMBARD: Will Spain think so? Will Rome?

O'NEILL: (*Very angry, in Tyrone accent*) I think so. And this is *my*
country. (*Quietly, in his usual accent*) I have married a very
talented, a very spirited, a very beautiful young woman. She
has left her people to join me here. They will never forgive
her for that. She is under this roof now, among a people she
has been reared to believe are wild and barbarous. I am
having a celebration tonight when I will introduce her to my
people. I particularly ask you two to welcome her here. But if
that is beyond you, I demand at least civility.

(*He leaves. Silence.* LOMBARD *begins gathering up his papers.*
HARRY *helps him. After a very long pause*:)

O'DONNELL: The bugger's off his aul head! – that's all there is to
it! She's turned the bugger's aul head.

HARRY: (*To* LOMBARD) Stay overnight. We can meet again
tomorrow morning.

O'DONNELL: And he let me blather on about the English building
new forts – and him jouking about the Newry fort all the
time! That's a class of treachery, Harry – that's what that is!

HARRY: You're talking rubbish, Hugh.

O'DONNELL: Do you know where the Butcher Bagenal was last
week? In the Finn valley. Raiding and plundering with a new
troop of soldiers over from Chester – the way you'd blood

young greyhounds! Slaughtered and beheaded fifteen families that were out saving hay along the river bank, men, women and children. With the result that at this moment there are over a hundred refugees in my mother's place in Donegal Town.

HARRY: (*To* LOMBARD) I'll have copies made of these.

O'DONNELL: I'll tell you something, Harry Hoveden: as long as he has that Upstart bitch with him, there'll be no welcome for him in Tyrconnell!

(LOMBARD *is about to leave with his papers*.)

HARRY: At least wait and meet her, Peter. For his sake.

(O'NEILL *enters, leading* MABEL *by the elbow*.)

an atmosphere

MABEL *is twenty, forthright, determined. Now she is very nervous. Her accent has traces of Staffordshire*.

O'NEILL: Here we are. I want you to meet two of my friends, Mabel. Hugh O'Donnell – Sir Hugh O'Donnell – Earl of Tyrconnell. My wife, Mabel.

MABEL: I'm pleased to meet you.

(*She holds out her hand*. O'DONNELL *has to take it. He does not speak. Pause*.)

O'NEILL: And Dr Peter Lombard, Titular Bishop of Armagh and Primate of All Ireland.

MABEL: I'm pleased to meet you. *silence*

(*Again she holds out her hand. After a pause* LOMBARD *takes it. He does not speak. Pause*.)

O'NEILL: We've got to keep on the right side of Peter: he's writing our history. *?– mabel*

LOMBARD: That seems to make you uneasy for some reason.

O'NEILL: Not as long as you tell the truth.

LOMBARD: You keep insisting on this 'truth', Hugh.

O'NEILL: Don't you believe in the truth, Archbishop?

LOMBARD: I don't believe that a period of history – a given space of time – my life – your life – that it contains within it one 'true' interpretation just waiting to be mined. But I do believe that it may contain within it several possible narratives: the life of Hugh O'Neill can be told in many

Lomb - disappointed? (handwritten)

different ways. And those ways are determined by the needs
and the demands and the expectations of different people
and different eras. What do they want to hear? How do they
want it told? So that in a sense I'm not altogether my own
man, Hugh. To an extent I simply fulfil the needs, satisfy the
expectations – don't I? *for a purpose* (handwritten)

(LOMBARD *turns away.*)

HARRY: You're looking rested now.

O'NEILL: And Harry Hoveden you know.

MABEL: Oh yes. I know Harry.

HARRY: Do you like the flowers?

MABEL: Yes, they're lovely.

O'NEILL: Broom.

MABEL: Yes.

O'NEILL: Spanish broom.

MABEL: Yes.

O'NEILL: Member of the *genista* family.

MABEL: Ah. I wouldn't know that.

O'NEILL: Actually that's Spanish broom . . . comes from Spain.
They need plenty of water.

MABEL: Broom? No, they don't. They need hardly any water at all.

(O'NEILL *looks accusingly at* HARRY.)

O'DONNELL: I'll have another slug of that wine – if that's all right
with you, Hugh.

O'NEILL: Of course. Anybody else?

(*Silence.*)

HARRY: Did you have a rest?

MABEL: I lay down but I didn't sleep any – I was too excited.
Everything's so . . . And the noise of those cows! I mean, I
looked out the window and all I could see was millions of
culture (handwritten) them stretching away to the hills. I mean, I never saw so
many cows in one place in all my life. There must be millions
of them. Cows and horses.

HARRY: We're moving you into the bedroom just above us. It's
quieter there.

LOMBARD: If you'll pardon me. I've some letters to write.

O'NEILL: The celebration begins at nine, Peter.

(LOMBARD *exits.*)

HARRY: (*Taking* O'DONNELL's *elbow*) And Hugh hasn't eaten since this morning.

O'DONNELL: What are you talking about? I ate only –

HARRY: We'll join you later.

> (*He steers* O'DONNELL *out in front of him. The moment they are alone* O'NEILL *grabs* MABEL *from behind and buries his face in her neck and hair.*)

MABEL: Oh, my God.

O'NEILL: Put your arms around me.

MABEL: I'm trembling all over.

O'NEILL: I want you now.

MABEL: 'Come and meet two friends,' you said.

O'NEILL: Now! – now! – now!

MABEL: You should have warned me, Hugh.

O'NEILL: Let's go upstairs.

MABEL: I'm in pieces, I am! Hugh O'Donnell and a popish priest all in a couple of minutes! Did you not see my hand? – it was shaking!

O'NEILL: I want to devour you.

MABEL: Our Henry calls him the Butcher O'Donnell. He says he strangles young lambs with his bare hands.

O'NEILL: That's true.

MABEL: Oh God! Are you serious?

O'NEILL: And eats them raw.

MABEL: Oh God! – you're not serious?

O'NEILL: We all do that here.

MABEL: Stop it, Hugh. And he speaks so funny! Why doesn't he speak like you?

O'NEILL: How do I speak?

MABEL: 'How do I speak?' – like those Old English nobs in Dublin.

O'NEILL: (*Tyrone accent*) That's why you're fair dying about me.

MABEL: And I met a popish priest, Hugh! That's the first time in my life I ever even *saw* one of them! And I said, 'I'm pleased to meet you'! Oh, my God, wait till my sister Mary hears this!

O'NEILL: And your brother Henry.

MABEL: Our Henry would shoot me, Hugh!

O'NEILL: Would he?

MABEL: You know he would! I shook the hand of a popish priest!

O'NEILL: An archbishop.

MABEL: Is that worse?

O'NEILL: Much worse. And look at it.

MABEL: At what?

O'NEILL: Your hand.

(*She looks at her hand.*)

It's turning black.

MABEL: It's – ?!

playful

(*She suddenly realizes she has been fooled. She gives a great
whoop of laughter and punches him.*)

childish

Oh, my God, I actually looked! You're a bastard, Hugh
O'Neill – that's what you are – a real bastard! (*She laughs
again, this time on the point of tears.*) Oh, my God, it's a bit too
much, Hugh . . . I think maybe – I think maybe I'm going to
cry – and the stupid thing is that I never ever cry . . . All that
secrecy – running away – the wedding ceremony – all the
excitement – being here – meeting those people . . . (*Now
crying*) They weren't very welcoming, Hugh – were they? I
mean they couldn't even speak to me – could they?

caught

O'NEILL: Give them time.

MABEL: Just when I was riding away from home I turned round
and there was my father looking out the landing window.
And he smiled and waved – he had no idea I was running
away. And he'll never understand why I did. He's a good
man and a fair-minded man and he'll try; but it will never
make sense to him. And he's going to be puzzled and hurt for
the rest of his life.

O'NEILL: Shhhh.

MABEL: I'm all right. Just a little bit confused, Hugh. Just a little
bit nervous. Everything's so different here. I knew it would
be strange – I knew that. But I didn't think it would be so
. . . foreign. I'm only fifty miles from home but I feel very far
away from everything I know.

O'NEILL: Give me your hand.

MABEL: It's not black. I'll be all right, Hugh. Just give me time.
We're a tough breed, the Upstarts.

O'NEILL: I have a present for you.

MABEL: Yes?

18

Universalises — new
marriages scary

O'NEILL: It's a new invention – a time-piece you carry around
    with you. It's called a watch.

MABEL: A what?

O'NEILL: A watch. You wear it on your finger just like a ring.

MABEL: Where did you get that thing?

O'NEILL: I had it made for you in London; specially.

MABEL: Oh, Hugh –

O'NEILL: The only other person I know who has one is Queen
    Elizabeth. *gift for for Queen*

MABLE: It's a beautiful thing, Hugh, really beautiful.

O'NEILL: Elizabeth wears it on this finger.

MABEL: The Queen has one! And I have the only other one!
    Queen Elizabeth and Countess Mabel – why not?

O'NEILL: Why not indeed?

MABEL: It really is beautiful. Thank you. Thank you very much.
    (*She kisses him.*) I'm sorry, Hugh. I'll never cry like that
    again. That's a promise. Never again. Ever. We're a tough
    breed, the O'Neills. *Contrast*
    (*Quick black.*) *caught*

SCENE 2

Almost a year has passed. The same room as in scene 1, but MABEL
*has added to the furnishings and the room is now more comfortable and
more colourful.*

MABEL *is sitting alone doing delicate and complicated lacework. She
works in silence for some time. Then from offstage the sudden and
terrifying sound of a young girl shrieking. This is followed immediately
by boisterous laughter, shouting, horseplay and a rapid exchange in
Irish between a young girl and a young man.*

MABEL *is terrified by the shriek. She drops her lacework. Her eyes are
shut tight. She sits frozen in terror for a few seconds – even when it is
obvious that the screaming is horseplay. Then in sudden fury she jumps
to her feet and goes to the exit left. As she goes – and unseen by her –
her sister* MARY *enters right.* MARY BAGENAL *is slightly older than*
MABEL. *Like* MABEL *there is a hint of Staffordshire in her accent.
And like* MABEL *she is a determined young woman.* *Contrast*

caught

MABEL: (*At exit*) Shut up out there! D'you hear me? Just shut up!
If you want to behave like savages, go on back to the bogs!
(*She is suddenly aware – and embarrassed – that* MARY *has
overheard her outburst.*)
Just horseplay. You would think they were killing each
other, wouldn't you? And I'm wasting my breath because
they don't understand a word of English.
(*There is an awkward silence.* MABEL *picks up her lacework.*)

MARY: They're getting my carriage ready. It's a long way back to
Newry.

MABEL: It's only fifty miles.

MARY: I suppose that's all.

MABEL: (*Impulsively*) Stay the night, Mary.

MARY: I can't.

MABEL: Please. For my sake. Please.

MARY: I'd like to, Mabel; you know I would but –

MABEL: Just one night.

MARY: If I'm not home before dark – you know our Henry – he'd
be worried sick.

MABEL: Let him worry about you for a change.

MARY: I really can't, Mabel. Not this time. Anyhow you and I
always fight after a few hours.

MABEL: Do we?

MARY: Well . . . sometimes.   *Transferable*
                                    dialogue

MABEL: In that case . . .

MARY: Next time . . . maybe.

MABEL: Next time.

MARY: That's a promise.
(*Another brief burst of shrieking and horseplay off. The sisters
smile uneasily at each other. Pause.*)
I left a box of nectarine and quince in your pantry. And a few
jars of honey. Last year's I'm afraid. If it crystallizes just dip
it in warm water.

MABEL: Thank you.
(*Pause*)   *what dont have*

MARY: They have no bees here, have they?

MABEL: No, we haven't.

MARY: I've finally persuaded our Henry to move his hives away from the house, thank heavens. Do you remember – just beyond the vegetable garden? – where father built the fishpond? – that's where they are now. In a semicircle round the pond.

MABEL: Yes.

MARY: He has over a hundred hives now.

MABEL: Has he?

MARY: Maybe more.

MABEL: Really?

MARY: We sold about four thousand pounds of honey last year. To the army mostly. They would buy all he can produce but they don't always pay him.

(*Pause.*)

And do you remember that bog land away to the left of the pond? Well, you wouldn't recognize that area now. We drained it and ploughed it and fenced it; and then planted a thousand trees there in four separate areas: apple and plum and damson and pear. Henry had them sent over from Kent. They're doing beautifully.

MABEL: Good.

MARY: They have no orchards here, have they?

MABEL: No, we haven't.

MARY: Mostly vegetable growing, is it?

MABEL: We go in for pastoral farming – not husbandry; cattle, sheep, horses. We have two hundred thousand head of cattle here at the moment – as you have heard. Did you say something about a herb garden?

MARY: Oh, that's a great success. That little square where we used to have the see-saw – do you remember that patch outside the kitchen window?

MABEL: I'm not gone a year, Mary.

MARY: Sorry. I've brought you some seeds. (*She produces envelopes from her bag.*) I've labelled them for you. (*Reads:*) Fennel. Lovage. Tarragon. Dill. Coriander. Borage. I had tansy, too, but I'm afraid it died on me. Do you remember every Easter we used to make tansy pudding and leave it – Sorry. Don't plant the fennel near the dill or the two will cross-fertilize.

21

MABEL: Is that bad? *caught*

MARY: You'll end up with a seed that's neither one thing or the other. Borage likes the sun but it will survive wherever you plant it – it's very tough. I should have some valerian seeds later in the year. I'll send you some. Are you still a bad sleeper? *calm her*

MABEL: Was father conscious at the end?

MARY: Father? Conscious? You should have heard him! Leaving personal messages for everybody – *subtext*

MABEL: Messages?

MARY: And detailed instructions about everything. The west door of the fort needs new hinges. The last consignment of muskets has defective hammers. Never depend totally on London because they don't really understand the difficult job we're doing over here.

MABEL: Personal messages? *subtext*

MARY: He forgot nobody. I'm to take up book-binding if you don't mind! Henry spends too much time at paperwork and not enough at soldiering. Old Tom, the gardener, should rub beeswax into his arthritic joints. Give a new Bible to the two maids from Tandragee. Half an hour before he died he asked what price we were getting for our eggs! Wonderful, wasn't it? *dig at mabel*

MABEL: Yes.

MARY: I miss him terribly, Mabel. I know he had a hard life but it was a very full life. You forget that almost single-handed he tamed the whole of County Down and County Armagh and brought order and prosperity to them. And God blessed his great endeavours; and Dad knew that, too. And that was a great consolation to him at the end. (*Pause.*) To all of us. (*Pause.*) So. (*Pause.*) I miss you so much, Mabel.

subtext savages

MABEL: I miss you, too.

MARY: I locked your bedroom door the day you left and it hasn't been opened since. But the house seems to be getting even bigger and emptier.

MABEL: You enjoy the garden, don't you?

MARY: Henry says I should get out more – meet more people. Where am I supposed to go out to? We're surrounded by the

mabel

Irish. And every day more and more of their hovels spring up all along the perimeter of our lands.

MABEL: You visit the Freathys, don't you?

MARY: They left. Months ago. Back to Cornwall.

MABEL: Why?

MARY: Couldn't take any more, I suppose. The nearest neighbour we have now is Patrick Barnewall of Rathfriland and that's fifteen miles away.

MABEL: But think of the welcome you always get from Young Patrick! Remember the day he said to you: (*lisps*) 'Mith Mary, come down to the old millhouse with me.' God, we laughed at that for weeks. Do you remember?

MARY: Yes.

MABEL: It became a kind of catchphrase with us – 'Mith Mary' – do you remember?

(MARY *cries quietly*.)

Here. Come on. We'll have none of that.

MARY: He was sixty-five last week, Young Patrick Barnewall.

MABEL: Are you all right, Mary?

MARY: He wants to marry me, Mabel. I told him I'd think about it.

MABEL: Oh, Mary, you – !

MARY: And I *am* thinking seriously about it.

MABEL: Mary, he's an old – !

MARY: I promised him I'd give him my answer next month. Our Henry thinks very highly of him.

MABEL: Mary, you can't marry Patrick Barnewall.

MARY: We'll see. I'm not sure yet. I think I will.

MABEL: The man's an old fool, Mary! He was always a fool! He has been a joke to us all our years!

MARY: He's still one of us, Mabel. And whatever about his age, he's a man of great honour. (*Now formal and distant*) Once more – it's time I was going. I've left nothing behind me, have I? Did you see my new horses? Of course you did. Aren't they handsome? Henry got them from Wales for my birthday. They're very sure-footed and they have tremendous stamina. You'll give my regards to Hugh?

MABEL: I don't know where he's got to. He'll be sorry to have missed you.

23

MARY: No, he won't. The twice we met we fought bitterly. I'll try
to come again, Mabel – if I get a chance. But you know how
angry Henry is.

MABEL: Is he still?

MARY: He still talks about taking you home by force.

MABEL: This is my home, Mary.

(The sudden shrieking as before. MARY *moves beside her and
speaks with concern and passion.)*

Insh savages

MARY: No, it's not. This can never be your home. Come away
with me now, Mabel.

MABEL: Please, Mary –

MARY: Yes, I know they have their colourful rituals and their
interesting customs and their own kind of law. But they are
not civilized, Mabel. And you can never trust them – you
must know that now – how treacherous and treasonable they
are – and steeped in religious superstition.

MABEL: That's enough, Mary.

MARY: You talk about 'pastoral farming' – what you really mean
is no farming – what you really mean is neglect of the land.
And a savage people who refuse to cultivate the land God
gave us have no right to that land.

MABEL: Stop that at once, Mary!

MARY: I'm sure some of them are kind and decent and
trustworthy. Of course they are. And yes – I know – Hugh is
different – Hugh was educated in England. But his people
are doomed in spite of their foreign friends and their popish
plotting because their way of life is doomed. And they are
doomed because civility is God's way, Mabel, and because
superstition must yield before reason. You know in your
heart what I'm saying is true. caught

MABEL: I became a Roman Catholic six months ago.

MARY: Oh God, Mabel, how could – ?!

MABEL: Out of loyalty to Hugh and to his people. As for civility I
believe that there is a mode of life here that is at least as
honourable and as cultivated as the life I've left behind. And
I imagine the Cistercian monks in Newry didn't think our
grandfather an agent of civilization when he routed them out
of their monastery and took it over as our home.

24

MARY: Hugh has two mistresses! – here! – now! – under this roof!
Is that part of his religion?

MABEL: That is part of his culture.

MARY: For God's sake! Is it part of his culture that he bows and
scrapes before the Lord Deputy in Dublin and promises
obedience and loyalty for life – and the very next day he's
plotting treason with Spain?

MABEL: That is politics.

MARY: 'Politics'! Listen to yourself. You're becoming slippery
like them! You're beginning to talk like them, to think like
them! Hugh is a traitor, Mabel – to the Queen, to her
Deputy, to everything you and I were brought up to believe
in. Do you know what our people call him? The Northern
Lucifer – the Great Devil – Beelzebub! Hugh O'Neill is evil
incarnate, Mabel! You tell me he has twenty gold and velvet
suits – but I have seen him eating with his bare hands! You
tell me that he speaks three or four languages and that every
leader in Europe respects him – but I can tell you that –
(*She breaks off because* O'NEILL *enters with* HARRY.)

HARRY: The consignment of lead has arrived from England.

O'NEILL: Have you got the import licence?

HARRY: Here.

O'NEILL: Check the order forms against the customs papers and
see that – Mary!

MARY: Hello, Hugh.

O'NEILL: When did you arrive?

MARY: A few hours ago.

O'NEILL: Well, this is a surprise.

MARY: I'm just about to leave.
(*They shake hands.*)

O'NEILL: What's the hurry?

MABEL: She wants to get home before dark.

MARY: Hello, Harry.

HARRY: You're a stranger, Mary. How are you?
(*They shake hands.*)

MARY: I'm well, Harry. How are you?

HARRY: Fine, thank you, fine.

O'NEILL: Well, this is unexpected.

MABEL: Isn't she looking well?

O'NEILL: Indeed. And have the sisters had a good long gossip?

MABEL: We're about talked out – aren't we?

O'NEILL: And how's the Queen's Marshal?

MARY: Henry's well, thank you.

O'NEILL: Henry's well.

MARY: Yes.

O'NEILL: Good.

MARY: Yes. (*Pause.*) He's very well.

O'NEILL: Splendid. But disquieted, I imagine, by that little difficulty with Maguire down in Fermanagh?

MARY: I don't know anything about that, Hugh.

O'NEILL: Of course not; naturally; affairs of state. But he does have a problem there – or at least so we've heard, Harry, haven't we?

MARY: Henry doesn't discuss those things with me.

O'NEILL: The difficulty – as we understand it – is that London has asked Maguire to make a public profession of his loyalty and obedience – to 'come in' as they coyly phrase it, as in to come in out of the wilderness, the Gaelic wilderness, of course. Nothing more than a token gesture is asked for – the English, unlike us, never drive principles to embarrassing conclusions. For heaven's sake, I've made the gesture myself, haven't I, Harry? And I've brought young Hugh O'Donnell 'in'. And I assure you, Mary, it means nothing, nothing. And in return for that symbolic . . . courtesy London offers you formal acknowledgement and recognition of what you already are – leader of your own people! Politically quaint, isn't it?

MARY: So taking a solemn oath of loyalty to Her Majesty is neither solemn nor binding to you, Hugh?

O'NEILL: Good heavens, no! I'm loyal today – disloyal tomorrow – you know how capricious we Gaels are. Anyhow, where was I? Yes, our friend Maguire. Maguire is having difficulty making that little courtesy. And so London gets peevish. And heated messages are exchanged. And terrible threats are made. And who gets hauled in to clean up the mess? Of course – poor old Henry! It's

26

always the Henrys, the menials in the middle, who get the
kicks, isn't it?

MARY: Our Henry's well able to handle rebels like Maguire.

O'NEILL: 'Our Henry'? Nobody better. London couldn't have a
more dutiful servant than Our Henry. As you and I know
well – but as London keeps forgetting – it's the plodding
Henrys of this world who are the real empire-makers. But
the point I'm getting to – (*To* HARRY) I'm not being
indiscreet, Harry, am I? – the reason I mention the problem
at all is that Maguire has thrown the head up and proclaims
he'll fight to the death before a syllable of loyalty to a foreign
queen will ever issue from his pure lips! I know. I know.
Trapped in the old Gaelic paradigms of thought. It's so
familiar – and so tedious. But then what does he do? Comes
to me who has already made the token gesture, me, the
'compromised' O'Neill in his eyes, comes to me and begs me
to fight beside him! Now! Look at the dilemma that places
me in, Mary. You do appreciate my dilemma, don't you?

MARY: I don't want to hear anything about this, Hugh.

O'NEILL: I try to live at peace with my fellow chieftains, with
your people, with the Old English, with Dublin, with
London, because I believe – I know – that the slow, sure tide
of history is with me, Mary. All I have to do is . . . just sit –
and – wait. And then a situation like this arises and how am I
to conduct myself?

MABEL: It's time Mary set off.

O'NEILL: Do I keep faith with my oldest friend and ally,
Maguire, and indeed with the Gaelic civilization that he
personifies? Or do I march alongside the forces of Her
Majesty? And I've marched with them before, Mary. You
didn't know that? Oh yes, I've trotted behind the Tudors on
several expeditions against the native rebels. I've even fought
alongside Our Henry in one little skirmish – oh, years and
years ago, when you and Mabel were still playing with your
dolls. Oh, yes, that's a detail our annalists in their wisdom
choose to overlook, perhaps because they believe, like Peter
Lombard, that art has precedence over accuracy. I'm
beginning to wonder should we trust historians at all!

27

Anyhow back to Maguire – and my dilemma. It really is a nicely balanced equation. The old dispensation – the new dispensation. My reckless, charming, laughing friend, Maguire – or Our Henry. Impulse, instinct, capricious genius, brilliant improvisation – or calculation, good order, common sense, the cold pragmatism of the Renaissance mind. Or to use a homely image that might engage you: pasture – husbandry. But of course I'm now writing a cliché history myself, amn't I? Because we both know that the conflict isn't between caricatured national types but between two deeply opposed civilizations, isn't it? We're really talking about a life-and-death conflict, aren't we? Only one will survive. You wouldn't disagree with that, would you?

MABEL: Mary wants to leave, Hugh.

O'NEILL: No, no, it's a nice point and I would welcome Mary's wholesome wisdom. I'll be very direct. Do I grasp the Queen's Marshal's hand? – using Our Henry as a symbol of the new order which every aristocratic instinct in my body disdains but which my intelligence comprehends and indeed grudgingly respects – because as a boy I spent nine years in England where I was nursed at the very wellspring of that new order – think of all those formative years in the splendid homes of Leicester and Sidney and indeed at the Court itself – hence the grand accent, Mary –

MABEL: Hugh, I think –

O'NEILL: No – allow me – or – or do I grip the hand of the Fermanagh rebel and thereby bear public and imprudent witness to a way of life that my blood comprehends and indeed loves and that is as old as the Book of Ruth. My dilemma. Help me, Mary. Which hand do I grasp? Because either way I make an enemy. Either way I interfere with that slow sure tide of history. No, that's unfair. I mustn't embarrass you. Let's put it another way. Which choice would history approve? Or to use the Archbishop's language: if the future historian had a choice of my two alternatives, which would he prefer for his acceptable narrative? Tell me.

MARY: I don't know anything about history, Hugh.

O'NEILL: All right; then which hand do I grasp?

28

MARY: Queen Elizabeth made you an Earl. And you accepted that title. And you know that that title carries with it certain duties and responsibilities.

O'NEILL: Those duties I have honoured faithfully.

MARY: Then as long as you continue to do that, Hugh, and if you are at peace with your conscience, you have no dilemma.

O'NEILL: (*To* HARRY) She's right, you know. (*To* MARY) A wise answer that, Mary. You have an admirably tidy little mind. That's what I'll do. And hope that history's approval and the guidance of my conscience are in accord.

(MARY *gathers her belongings together. She embraces* MABEL.)

MARY: I'm glad to see you looking so well.

MABEL: Write to me.

(*They kiss.*)

Thank you for all you brought. — poungant

MARY: I'll not forget the valerian. Goodbye, Harry.

HARRY: Safe journey, Mary.

(*They shake hands.*)

MARY: Goodbye, Hugh.

(HUGH *is examining the seed packets with excessive interest.*)

O'NEILL: Sorry? humiliating

MARY: Goodbye.

O'NEILL: Oh – goodbye – goodbye – remember me to Our Henry.

(*Both women exit. Long pause.*) ironic

HARRY: All that will go straight back to the Marshal.

O'NEILL: What's that, Harry?

HARRY: Everything you said will be reported to Bagenal – and to London.

O'NEILL: That's why I told her.

HARRY: You want it known that you've promised Maguire you'd help him?

O'NEILL: I don't think I told her that, did I? (*Reads:*) 'The coriander seed. Watch this seed carefully as it ripens suddenly and will fall without warning.' Sounds like Maguire, doesn't it? – Coriander Maguire.

HARRY: Because if you renege on that promise he certainly will fall.

O'NEILL: What herb are you, Harry? What about dill? 'Has a

comforting and soothing effect.' Close enough. And who is borage? 'Inclined to induce excessive courage, even recklessness.' That's O'Donnell, isn't it? Borage O'Donnell.

HARRY: Or are you saying that you're going to take the English side against Maguire, Hugh?

(O'NEILL *gathers the envelopes of seeds together*.)

In fact are you going to betray your old friend, Maguire?

O'NEILL: (*Roars*) 'Betray my old – '! For Christ's sake don't you start using language like that to me, Harry! (*Softly*) Maguire is a fool. He's determined to rise up and nobody can stop him and he'll be hacked to pieces and his people routed and his country planted with Upstarts and safe men. It happened to Fitzmaurice. And McDermott. And Nugent. And O'Reilly. And O'Connor. And O'Kelly. Their noble souls couldn't breathe another second under 'tyranny'. And where are they now? Wiped out. And what did they accomplish? Nothing. But because of their nobility, survival – basic, crude, day-to-day survival – is made infinitely more difficult for the rest of us.

HARRY: You are unfair to Maguire, Hugh. He's impetuous but he's no fool.

O'NEILL: I know – I know – of course I know Maguire's no fool. Maguire has no choice. Maguire has to rise. History, instinct, his decent passion, the composition of his blood – he has no alternative. So he will fulfil his fate. It's not a tragic fate and it's not a heroic fate. But his open embrace of it has elements of both, I suppose. Of course I know all that, for Christ's sake . .

(O'DONNELL *bursts in. He is breathless with excitement*.)

O'DONNELL: News, boys! News! News! News! Wait till you hear the news, Hugh! Big news – huge news – enormous news! Sorry for bursting in on you like this, Harry. Peter Lombard's with me. We've been riding since dawn. God, I'm wild dry – give us a swig of that wine, Harry. This is it, Hugh boy! I'm telling you – this is it!

O'NEILL: This is what?

O'DONNELL: Don't ask me. I can't tell you. Wait for Peter – I can't spoil it on him. But I'll say this much, Hugh O'Neill: I never thought I'd live to see the day! (*Accepts glass.*) Decent man, Harry. (*Toasts*) To the future – to a great, great future – to the three of us – (*Enter* LOMBARD.) – to the four of us! (*To* LOMBARD) I haven't opened my mouth – have I?

(LOMBARD *is equally excited but controlled. He shakes hands with* O'NEILL *and then* HARRY.)

LOMBARD: Hugh. Good to see you.

O'NEILL: Welcome, Peter.

LOMBARD: Harry. (*To* O'NEILL) I was going to send a messenger but I thought it was much too important.

O'DONNELL: Spout it out, Peter!

LOMBARD: It really is astonishing news, Hugh.

O'NEILL: It's Spain, isn't it?

O'DONNELL: The aul wizard. I never said a word.

LOMBARD: It's Spain, Hugh. After all these years. God be praised a thousand times. It is indeed Spain.

O'DONNELL: Can you believe it?

LOMBARD: Years of begging, cajoling, arguing – years of hoping – years of despairing.

O'DONNELL: Years of praying, Peter.

LOMBARD: Years of praying indeed. But he has kept his promises, Hugh. Don Francisco Gómez de Sandoval y Rojas, Fifth Marquis of Denia, Duke of Lerma, my friend, Ireland's friend, he has kept his promise.

O'DONNELL: Lerma determines their foreign policy.

(O'NEILL *moves away and stands alone downstage.*)

HARRY: This isn't the first time Lerma has made promises.

LOMBARD: Passed by the Council of State last Thursday week. Signed by King Philip himself the following morning. This isn't a promise. This is guaranteed. And solid. And substantial.

O'DONNELL: Yipeeeeee!

LOMBARD: At this moment they are mustering an army and assembling a fleet.

O'DONNELL: Do you see those wee Spanish soldiers in the field, Harry? Bloody ferrets! Jesus, they'd go down a rabbit hole to get you!

HARRY: How solid? How substantial?

O'N –silent
reflecting

31

LOMBARD: At least thirty-five ships – galleons, men-of-war and some hundred-ton vessels.

HARRY: Where are they going to land? - details

LOMBARD: I don't know. That's a military matter.

HARRY: But it's crucial. It has got to be somewhere along the north coast. true

LOMBARD: I think I heard some mention of Kinsale.

O'DONNELL: Wherever that is. Never heard of it.

HARRY: Kinsale's out of the question. We'd have to march an army through the full length of the country to join forces with them. (*To* O'NEILL) It can't be Kinsale, Hugh.

sense
doom

LOMBARD: Then tell them it can't be Kinsale.

HARRY: Who's the commander-in-chief ?

LOMBARD: Don Juan del Aguila.

O'DONNELL: Whoever he is. Don Hugho del Ballyshannon's for more wine, boys!

HARRY: Tell me about Aguila.

LOMBARD: He's from the Barraco in the province of Avila. Not brilliant but very competent, very experienced.

HARRY: How many men?

LOMBARD: At least six thousand.

HARRY: Not enough.

LOMBARD: They'll be fully trained and equipped; and it's up to us to match that number. (*To* O'NEILL) You and Hugh here have got to tour the whole country and whip every Gaelic chieftain into shape.

HARRY: Where are they mustering their men?

LOMBARD: Most of them are Spanish but they hope to levy a few companies of Italians.

O'DONNELL: Do you see those Italians? Bloody savages! The only time they ever smile is when they're sinking a sword in you! Jesus, Hugh, we'll go through the English quicker than a physic!

(MABEL *enters.* O'DONNELL *embraces her warmly.*)

We're up, Mabel darling! We're up and the Spanish are beside us!

(*She looks at* O'NEILL.)

LOMBARD: Forgive, us, Mabel. We're a bit elated.

MABEL: The Spanish are coming?

O'DONNELL: Lift up your heart, Dark Rosie!

LOMBARD: The Spanish are coming. At long last. And there's more, Hugh [O'NEILL]. There's still more.

O'DONNELL: Belt it out, Archbishop Lombard.

LOMBARD: A Bull of Indulgence from His Holiness Pope Clement VIII.

O'DONNELL: Quiet! Quiet! Let the dog see the rabbit!

LOMBARD: (*Reads*) 'To the archbishops, bishops, prelates, chiefs, earls, barons and people of Ireland. Encouraged by the exhortations of our predecessors and ourself you have long struggled to recover and preserve your liberty and to throw off the yoke of slavery imposed on you by the English, deserters from the Holy Roman Church. Now, to all of you who follow and assist our beloved son, Hugh O'Neill, and the Catholic army, if you truly repent and confess and if possible receive the Holy Communion, we grant plenary pardon and remission of all sins, as usually granted to those setting out to the war against the Turks for the recovery of the Holy Land. Rome. The Ninth Year of Our Pontificate.'

O'DONNELL: Jesus, great word that – 'pontificate'.

LOMBARD: Which means, Hugh, that now you aren't fighting a mere war – you are fighting a holy crusade.

O'DONNELL: Goddamn bloody right, Peter!

LOMBARD: Which means, too, that we are no longer a casual grouping of tribes but a nation state united under the Papal colours.

O'DONNELL: Is that big enough news for you, man – eh?
(*Everybody looks at* O'NEILL. *Silence. He walks slowly across the room.*)
Hi! Hugh!
(*Silence.*)
(*To others*) What's wrong with the bugger? (*To* O'NEILL) O'Neill! Sir Hugh! Tyrone! Did you hear what the man's just said?

O'NEILL: Yes; yes, I heard.

O'DONNELL: 'Yes, I heard'! What the hell's wrong with the bugger?

(*Silence. Then when* O'NEILL *finally speaks, he speaks very softly, almost as if he were talking to himself.*)

O'NEILL: I'm remembering Sir Henry Sidney and Lady Mary, may they rest in peace. We spent the winters in the great castle at Ludlow in Shropshire. I've few memories of the winters. It's the summers I remember and the autumns, in Kent, in the family seat at Penshurst. And the orchards; and the deerpark; and those enormous fields of wheat and barley. A golden and beneficent land. Days without blemish. Every young man's memories. And every evening after dinner Sir Henry would propose a topic for discussion: *Travel – Seditions and Troubles – Gardens – Friendship and Loyalty – Good Manners – The Planting of Foreign Countries*. And everyone round the table had to contribute – the family, guests, even myself, even his son Philip who was younger than I. And Sir Henry would tease out the ideas and guide the conversation almost imperceptibly but very skilfully so that by the time we rose from the table he had moulded the discourse into a well-rounded and formal essay on whatever the theme was. I was only a raw boy at the time but I was conscious not only that new ideas and concepts were being explored and fashioned but that I was being explored and fashioned at the same time. And that knowledge wasn't unflattering. Drake was there once, I remember. And Frobisher and his officers on the eve of their first South American voyage. Gross men; vain men. But Sir Henry's grace and tact seemed to transform all that naked brutality and imperial greed into boyish excitement and manly adventure. He was the only father I ever knew. I was closer to him and to Lady Mary than I was to O'Hagan who fostered me. I loved them both very much.

Anyhow, time came to come home. I was almost seventeen then. And the night before I left Lady Mary had an enormous farewell dinner for me – there must have been a hundred guests. And at the end of the meal Sir Henry got to his feet – I knew he was slightly drunk, maybe he was more drunk than I knew – and he said: 'Our disquisition tonight will explore a matter of some interest to England and of

particular interest to Master O'Neill who goes home
tomorrow to become a leader of his people. And the
matter is this, and I quote from a letter I have just
received from my friend, Andrew Trollope. "Those
Irishmen who live like subjects play but as the fox which
when you have him on a chain will seem tame; but if he
ever gets loose, he will be wild again." So. Speak to that,
Fox O'Neill.' *prophetic*
And then he laughed. And everybody joined in. And then
a hundred people were laughing at me . . .
I left the next morning before the household was awake.
And ever since – up until this minute – ever since, that
trivial little hurt, that single failure in years of courtesy has
pulsed relentlessly in a corner of my heart. Until now.
And now for no reason that pulse is quiet and all my
affection for Sir Henry returns without qualification.
(*Pause*.) But all that is of no interest to anybody but – Ind.
myself. *meet as equals* hist

O'DONNELL: Damned right it isn't. Bloody pulse? – what's he
blathering about? *lacks empathy*

(O'NEILL *claps his hands, dismissing the entire episode. He is
now suddenly very brisk and very efficient.*)

O'NEILL: The present. (*To* LOMBARD) You're right. Hugh and I
will tour the country to gather support. We'll set out next
Monday. (*To* O'DONNELL) No cap-in-hand. We go with
authority and assurance.

O'DONNELL: Damned right we do!

O'NEILL: (*To* HARRY) Get a letter off to Lerma today. Kinsale is
out of the question. If they insist on landing in the south –
anywhere in the south – tell them to cancel the expedition.
(*To* LOMBARD) What equipment are they bringing?

LOMBARD: Six battery pieces and six hundred hundredweight of
powder.

O'NEILL: (*To* HARRY) We'll need at least five hundred small guns.
Tell Lerma we're expert in guerrilla warfare but
inexperienced in open battle.

LOMBARD: And see that Archbishop Oviedo gets a copy – he's
very influential.

HARRY: Right.

LOMBARD: (*To* O'NEILL) The Pope has ordered him to sail in the *San Andrea* – that's the flagship.

O'DONNELL: Flagship! (*Salutes*.) Jesus, that word flagship's like music to me!

O'NEILL: They're bringing their own saddles?

LOMBARD: Yes; but they expect you to supply the horses.

O'NEILL: (*To* HARRY) A levy of five horses on every family. And oatmeal. And butter. (*To* LOMBARD) A Bull of Indulgence isn't enough. Everybody who opposes us must be publicly identified. I need a Bull of Excommunication.

LOMBARD: You won't get that, Hugh.

O'NEILL: We got one before.

LOMBARD: Twenty years ago.

O'NEILL: I want a Bull of Excommunication, Peter.

LOMBARD: I've tried. I'll try again. Oviedo's our only hope.

O'NEILL: (*To* HARRY) Messages to all the Ulster leaders: a meeting here the day after tomorrow – at noon.

HARRY: Noon.

O'NEILL: Send Brian O'Hagan across to the Earl of Argyle for mercenaries.

HARRY: How many?

O'NEILL: As many as he can get. And pay in advance.

HARRY: How much money will he need?

O'NEILL: Whatever Argyle asks. (*To* O'DONNELL) You're the expert on horses.

O'DONNELL: Bloody right.

O'NEILL: (*To* HARRY) Take him up to the upper meadows and show him the new stock. (*To* O'DONNELL) Pick only the horses that are strong enough for a long campaign.

O'DONNELL: How many are up there?

O'NEILL: Something over three thousand.

O'DONNELL: I'll have a look.

(HARRY *and* O'DONNELL *go to the door.* O'DONNELL *stops there.*)

With all the excitement I forgot to tell you the rumour that's going round Dublin: the Lord Deputy's about to proclaim you a traitor.

O'NEILL: That'll do no harm at all. Good. Excellent.

O'DONNELL: And do you know what they're offering as a reward for you? Go on – guess – guess.

O'NEILL: All right. Tell me.

O'DONNELL: £2000 alive, £1000 dead. The same as they were offering five years ago – for the shit O'Doherty!
(*He gives a great whoop and exits.*)

O'NEILL: (*To* LOMBARD) Your network of priests could be useful. How many are you in touch with?

LOMBARD: Twenty, twenty-five.

O'NEILL: Every week? Every month?

LOMBARD: It varies. They have a price on their head, too.

O'NEILL: Get in touch with them as soon as possible. Tell them I'll need them as messengers all over Europe.

LOMBARD: I'll do what I can.
(LOMBARD *goes to the door.*)

O'NEILL: And put Oviedo to work that Excommunication Bull.

LOMBARD: Oviedo can't demand it, Hugh. The decision is the Pope's. Excommunication is a spiritual matter.

O'NEILL: Don't play those games with me, Peter. The situation is as 'spiritual' now as it was twenty years ago. I need Excommunication for solidarity here, for solidarity with Europe. I expect you to deliver it.

LOMBARD: As I said, I've tried. I'll try again.
(*He leaves.* O'NEILL *goes to the desk and busies himself with papers. Silence.* MABEL *watches him for a while and then goes to him.*)

MABEL: Stop it, Hugh.

O'NEILL: Stop what?

MABEL: This Spanish business. Don't let it happen.

O'NEILL: Why should I do that?

MABEL: Because you know this isn't what you really want to happen.

O'NEILL: I've spent twenty years trying to bring it about, haven't I?

MABEL: This isn't your way.

O'NEILL: But you know what my way is.

MABEL: Calculation – deliberation – caution. You inch forward –

O'N doubh

37

you withdraw. You challenge – you retreat. You defy – you
submit. Every important move you have ever made has been
pondered for months.

O'NEILL: I have –

MABEL: That's why you're the most powerful man in Ireland:
you're the only Irish chieftain who understands the political
method. O'Donnell doesn't. Maguire doesn't. McMahon
doesn't. That's why the Queen is never *quite* sure how to deal
with you – you're the antithesis of what she expects a Gaelic
chieftain to be. That's your strength. And that's why your
instinct now is not to gamble everything on one big throw
that is more than risky.

O'NEILL: This time Spain is with us.

MABEL: Spain is using you.

O'NEILL: We're using each other. We've courted each other for
years.

MABEL: And that has given you some small negotiating power
with England. But the manoeuvrings are over now. And I
promise you, Hugh, England will throw everything she has
into this war.

O'NEILL: So will Spain.

MABEL: No, she won't. It's not Spain's war. It's your war. And
you're taking on a nation state that is united and determined
and powerful and led by a very resolute woman.

O'NEILL: Is there an echo of pride in that?

MABEL: Please, Hugh.

O'NEILL: Are we so inconsiderable? We aren't without
determination. We aren't disunited.

MABEL: Just look calmly at what you are.

O'NEILL: I know exactly what we are.

MABEL: You are not united. You have no single leader. You have
no common determination. At best you are an impromptu
alliance of squabbling tribesmen –

O'NEILL: Careful!

MABEL: – grabbing at religion as a coagulant only because they
have no other idea to inform them or give them cohesion.
(*Pause.*)

O'NEILL: Is that a considered abstract of the whole Gaelic history

38

and civilization, Mabel? Or is it nothing more than an honest-to-goodness, instant wisdom of the Upstart? (*He is instantly sorry and grabs her and holds her in his arms.*) I'm sorry, Mabel. Forgive me. I'm very sorry. I'm a bit on edge. (*Kisses the top of her head.*) Of course you're right. We have no real cohesion. And of course I'm worried. Even O'Donnell's enthusiasm worries me: for him it's all a huge adventure – cattle-raiding on an international scale. (MABEL *moves away*.) ~~diff. agenda?~~
~~And I never quite know what the Archbishop is thinking.~~

MABEL: He talks about a Catholic Confederation, a Catholic Army, about you leading Europe in a glorious Catholic Counter-Reformation. But I always have the feeling that when he's talking about you and about Ireland, he's really talking in code about Rome and Roman power. Is that unfair to him?

O'NEILL: I don't know.

MABEL: Just as Spain's only interest is in Spain and in Spanish power. But my only real concern is you, Hugh. This is not going to be just another skirmish at the edge of a forest. This is a war that England must win because her very survival is at stake. And all I know for sure is that, when the war is over, whatever the outcome, the Lombards and the Oviedos won't be here – they'll have moved on to more promising territories. (*Pause.*) I shouldn't have spoken. (*Pause.*) I didn't mean to intrude. (*Pause.*) I'm sure I don't really understand the overall thing.

O'NEILL: The overall thing.

MABEL: That's what matters in the end, isn't it?

O'NEILL: The overall thing – we don't even begin to know what it means.

(*Silence. She gathers her pieces of lace and goes to the door.*)

MABEL: Something Mary told me: a new Lord Deputy is about to be appointed, somebody called Lord Mountjoy. Henry says he's meticulous, and a ruthless fighter. Blount – that's his real name; Charles Blount. That's all she knows. Oh yes – he smokes a lot. It's all very secret. She made me swear not to tell you.

(*She is about to leave when she is arrested by the controlled passion of* O'NEILL's *voice.*)

O'NEILL: I have spent my life attempting to do two things. I have attempted to hold together a harassed and a confused people by trying to keep them in touch with the life they knew before they were overrun. It wasn't a life of material ease but it had its assurances and it had its dignity. And I have done that by acknowledging and indeed honouring the rituals and ceremonies and beliefs these people have practised since before history, long before the God of Christianity was ever heard of. And at the same time I have tried to open these people to the strange new ways of Europe, to ease them into the new assessment of things, to nudge them towards changing evaluations and beliefs. Two pursuits that can scarcely be followed simultaneously. Two tasks that are almost self-cancelling. But they have got to be attempted because the formation of nations and civilizations is a willed act, not a product of fate or accident. And for you to suggest that religion is the only coagulant that holds us together is to grossly and ignorantly overlook an age-old civilization. In one detail you are right: it is not my nature to gamble everything on one big throw –

MABEL: So have your war.

O'NEILL: But if I don't move now that civilization is certainly doomed.

MABEL: So go and fight. That's what you've spent your life doing. That's what you're best at. Fighting to preserve a fighting society. I don't care any more.

O'NEILL: Because you're not quite sure which side you're on?

MABEL: Why do you keep rejecting me, Hugh?

O'NEILL: I can see it wouldn't break your heart to see the Gaelic order wiped out. But let's look at what the altenative is: the buccaneering, vulgar, material code of the new colonials –

MABEL: (*Leaving*) Excuse me.

O'NEILL: The new 'civility' approved, we're told, by God Himself. Isn't that your coagulant – God? No, better still, God and trade. Now there's a combination.

40

(*She swings back and glares at him in hatred. He ignores her and pretends to busy himself at the desk.*)

MABEL: I want your mistresses out of this house immediately.

O'NEILL: (*Tyrone accent*) Aw, now sorry, ma'am.

MABEL: What does sorry mean?

O'NEILL: That my mistresses stay.

MABEL: I will not live in the same house as those – those harlots! Get those tramps out of here!

O'NEILL: No.

whats a hero?

MABEL: Then I go.

O'NEILL: That's your choice.

(*Pause. She tries not to cry.*)

MABEL: I'm pregnant, Hugh.

(O'NEILL *goes to the exit.*)

O'NEILL: (*Calls*) Harry! Have you a moment?

MABEL: Did you hear what I said?

(*He returns to the desk.*)

O'NEILL: That you're pregnant? Yes, I heard. So if all goes well – isn't that the expression? – if all goes well that will be ten legitimate children I'll have sired and about – what? – maybe thirty bastards. *subtext...*

MABEL: Oh, Hugh –

O'NEILL: Or so my people boast. An affectionate attribute every nation bestows on its heroes. *hero?*

(*Again he has instant remorse. As she runs to the door he runs after her.*)

Mabel! Mabel, I'm –

(O'DONNELL *dashes on.*)

O'DONNELL: A messenger from Spain outside, Hugh! (*To* MABEL) It gets better by the minute! (*To* O'NEILL) The Spanish fleet sails on September 3! (*To* MABEL) Maybe you speak Spanish? You should hear your man out there: 'Beeg fleet – beeg ships'!

O'NEILL: Where do they sail from?

O'DONNELL: Lisbon. On the first tide.

O'NEILL: And where do they land?

(HARRY *enters.*)

HARRY: Did you call me?

O'NEILL: Where do they land?

O'DONNELL: 'Keen–sall.'

O'NEILL: Where – where?

O'DONNELL: 'Keen–sall' – Kinsale, I suppose.

O'NEILL: Oh, God, no. *doom*

O'DONNELL: Wherever Kinsale is. This is it, Mabel darling! This is it! Yipeeeeee!

(*Quick black.*)

end-contrast

Ends-high

ACT 2

SCENE I

About eight months later. The edge of a thicket somewhere near the Sperrin mountains.

Exile unire

O'NEILL is on his knees. He is using a wooden box as a table and he is writing – scoring out – writing rapidly, with total concentration, almost frantically. Various loose pages on the ground beside him. He looks tired and anxious and harassed. He is so concentrated on his writing that he is unaware of O'DONNELL's entrance. Then, when he is aware, he reaches perfunctorily for the dagger at his side.

O'DONNELL, too, looks tired and anxious. He is also spattered with mud and his boots are sodden.

O'DONNELL: It's only me. I suppose you thought something had happened to me.

O'NEILL: You were longer than you thought.

O'DONNELL: I had to make detours going and coming back – the countryside's crawling with troops. And then there were a lot of things to see to at home – disputes – documents – the usual. Look at my feet. These Sperrins aren't mountains – they're bloody bogs! I suppose you wouldn't have a spare pair of boots?

O'NEILL: What you see is all I have.

O'DONNELL: I was afraid you might have had to move on to some new place.

O'NEILL: It's been very quiet here.

O'DONNELL: God, I'm exhausted.

(*He throws himself on the ground and spreads out in exhaustion. His eyes closed. O'NEILL continues writing. Silence.*)

O'NEILL: Have you any food?

(O'DONNELL *opens his leather bag and produces a scone of bread.* O'NEILL *goes to him, takes the bread and eats it hungrily.*)

O'DONNELL: My mother made me half-a-dozen of them but I met a family begging on the roadside near Raphoe. Everywhere you go there are people scavenging in the fields, hoking up

43

bits of roots, eating fistfuls of watercress. They look like
skeletons. Where's Mabel?

O'NEILL: Harry took her to relatives of Ruadhaire Dall O
Cathain's near Dungiven. She wasn't able to keep moving
about any more.

O'DONNELL: Proper order, too. When is she due?

O'NEILL: Next week probably. *contrast*

O'DONNELL: She's been terrific, Hugh. Not a whimper out of her
all these months – and us skulking about like tramps.

O'NEILL: I know.

O'DONNELL: Next week. Great. At least that'll be something to
celebrate. I'm wild dry. Have you any water?
(O'NEILL *hands him a bottle.*)

O'NEILL: Well?

O'DONNELL: I hate this aul brown Tyrone water – with all
respects. How do you drink it?

O'NEILL: What did you learn?

O'DONNELL: I never made Ballyshannon. Dowcra's troops were
waiting for me there. I got no further than Donegal Town.
My mother says to tell you she was asking for you.

O'NEILL: Well?

O'DONNELL: Well, it's a complete collapse, she says. The
countryside's in chaos, she says: slaughter, famine, disease.
There must be eight thousand people crowded into Donegal
Town looking for food.

O'NEILL: Where's Mountjoy?

O'DONNELL: Mountjoy's riding up and down the country and
beheading everything that stirs. And every week somebody
new caves in; and those that are holding out are being picked
off one after the other. But do you know what I heard? Jesus,
wait till you hear this, Hugh. We were betrayed at Kinsale!
They knew we were going to attack that morning. They were
sitting waiting for us. And do you know how they knew?
Brian Og McMahon slipped them the word! Time, place,
number of men, everything. And do you know how they
bought him? With a bottle of whiskey! Jesus, wouldn't it
break your heart? That's what they're all saying at home.
There could have been 10 million Spanish soldiers and we

still wouldn't have won. Because one of our own captains bloody well betrayed us.

O'NEILL: Rubbish.

O'DONNELL: What d'you mean – rubbish?

O'NEILL: All lies.

O'DONNELL: You don't believe me?

O'NEILL: You don't believe it yourself.

O'DONNELL: It's what everybody at home's saying . . . I don't know . . . maybe . . . but you'll agree those McMahons were always shifty buggers.

O'NEILL: How big is the collapse?

O'DONNELL: It's all over. It's all finished, Hugh.

O'NEILL: Who has submitted? Names.

O'DONNELL: My mother says they're crawling in on their hands and knees and offering hostages and money and whatnot. It would be easier to count the handful that are still holding out.

O'NEILL: Names.

O'DONNELL: Names . . . where do you begin? . . . all right, names . . . Jesus, I just hate saying them . . . Turlough McHenry of the Fews. The two Antrim O'Neills. O'Malley of Mayo. O'Flaherty of Annaly. Maguire of Fermanagh –

O'NEILL: Cuchonnacht?

O'DONNELL: God, no! The wee get, Connor Roe. Christ, man, aul Cuchonnacht's still dodging about the Lisnaskea area with fifteen picked men and hammering away every chance he gets! The McDevitts of Ballybeg, all of them, every branch of the family. The McSwineys of Fanad. Wouldn't it sicken you? – the bloody McSwineys that our family has kept and protected for generations and then when you're down in your luck. (*Suddenly brightening*) But do you know who's holding out? You'd never guess! Still the same wee maggot he always was but at least he hasn't caved in yet. The sheep-stealer! – the shit O'Doherty from Inishowen! Jesus, isn't it well we didn't slip him the Bordeaux Special that time?

O'NEILL: Go on.

O'DONNELL: O'Kelly of Kilconnell. Brave enough; he held out

45

until last Sunday and then do you know what he did? The aul eejit, Jesus, pompous as ever; he had this blond wig that an aul aunt had brought home from Paris. Anyhow he sticks the blond wig on his head, puts on a scarlet jacket, marches into Galway town and offers his surrender – in French! Poor aul bugger – trying to make a bit of a gesture out of it . . . Anyhow, one swing of an axe and the aul blond head was rolling about the street . . .

O'NEILL: Go on.

O'DONNELL: Who else? . . . O'Reilly of East Breffni. McWilliam Burke of Connaught. O'Kane –

O'NEILL: Which O'Kane?

O'DONNELL: Your daughter Rose's husband. Sure you always knew he was a bloody weed. Fitzmaurice of Kerry. Donnell McCarthy of Bandon. I can go on forever. O'Dowd. O'Dwyer of Kilnamanagh. God, Hugh, I'm telling you – it's endless.

(O'NEILL *picks up his papers and puts them in order. Silence.*)

O'NEILL: Where's Chichester?

O'DONNELL: He's taken over your place at Dungannon.

O'NEILL: Hah!

O'DONNELL: He controls the whole of East Ulster. Dowcra controls the whole of West Ulster. Carew controls the whole of Munster. And Mountjoy controls the whole country. (*Pause.*) He did a kind of a dirty thing last week, Mountjoy.

(O'NEILL *stops and looks at him.*)

He smashed the O'Neill crowning stone at Tullyhogue. There was no call for that, was there? (*Pause.*) What else is there? The King of France has written to Elizabeth to come to terms with us. Wasting his bloody time. All your Derry lands have been given to Bishop Montgomery and your Armagh lands to the new Protestant bishop there . . . I don't think I heard anything else . . . they've taken over your fishing rights on the Bann and the Foyle . . . And I've resigned, Hugh.

O'NEILL: What do you mean?

O'DONNELL: Handed over to the brother, Rory.

O'NEILL: Oh, Hugh.

O'DONNELL: And I'm leaving at the end of the week.

O'NEILL: Where for?

O'DONNELL: I don't know. Wherever the ship takes me. Maybe Spain.

(*Pause.* O'DONNELL *smiles resolutely and uncertainly.*)

No, it's not a sudden decision. I've been thinking about it for months, ever since Kinsale. And Rory'll be a fine chieftain – he's a solid man, very calm, very balanced. He hasn't my style or flair, of course; but then I have a fault or two, as you know. The blood gets up too easy and I was always useless at dealing with civil servants and Lord Deputies and people like that. Not like you. Even with my own people, for God's sake: the bloody McSwineys of Fanad couldn't wait to get a thump at me. Anyhow the chieftain isn't all that important – isn't that what our bards tell us? The land is the goddess that every ruler in turn is married to. We come and we go but she stays the same. And the Tyrconnell goddess is getting a new man. Trouble is, no matter who she's married to, I'll always be in love with her . . . (*Takes a drink of water.*) Jesus, that stuff would physic an elephant!

O'NEILL: When are you leaving?

O'DONNELL: Next Friday.

O'NEILL: Where from?

O'DONNELL: I'm getting a ship at a place called Castlehaven – wherever that is.

O'NEILL: Near Skibbereen.

O'DONNELL: Wherever Skibbereen is.

O'NEILL: You'll be back, Hugh.

O'DONNELL: Aye. In a blond wig and a scarlet jacket and leading a hundred thousand Spaniards! And next time we'll land in Derry – better still Rathmullan and my mother'll get landing fees from the buggers – right? (*Laughs.*) No, it's all over, Hugh. Finished for all time. Poor aul Peter Lombard, terrible bleak ending for his history, isn't it? I mean, Jesus, how can the poor man make an interesting story out of a defeat like this – eh? If he'd any sense he'd scrap the whole thing. Yes, there is one thing that might

47

bring me home sometime – to get my sheep back from the
shit O'Doherty. Oh, man . . .

(*Impulsively, about to break down, he flings his arms around*
O'NEILL. *They embrace for several seconds. Then* O'DONNELL
goes to his bag for a handkerchief.)

What about you? What are you going to do?

O'NEILL: I don't have many choices. And I'm not as young as you.

O'DONNELL: Damned right – twenty years older at least.

O'NEILL: My instinct is to leave like you.

O'DONNELL: What does Mabel think?

O'NEILL: She's urging me to hang on, pick up the pieces, start all
over again. They're very tenacious, the New English.

O'DONNELL: Maybe she's right. She's a very loyal wee girl.

O'NEILL: Her reasoning is that since the country is in such
anarchy Mountjoy has neither the energy nor the resources
to impose order; but if I were to make a public declaration of
loyalty to the Queen and if she were to reinstate me –

O'DONNELL: Are you out of your – ?!

O'NEILL: With only nominal authority, without political or
military power whatever, then Mabel says I should accept
almost any conditions, no matter how humiliating, as long as
I'd be restored to my base again and to my own people.

O'DONNELL: And why in God's name would Elizabeth restore
you?

O'NEILL: Because she knows that the only way she can rule
Ireland at this point is by *using* someone like me. She hates
me – but she can rule through me provided she has control
over me. At least that's Mabel's argument. I think I could get
enough of my people behind me and she thinks some of the
New English would back it – those that are sick of England.

O'DONNELL: So you're writing your submission?

O'NEILL: What's the alternative? The life of a soured émigré
whingeing and scheming round the capitals of Europe.

O'DONNELL: Like me.

O'NEILL: I didn't mean that, Hugh.

O'DONNELL: Show me that. You know, you're a tenacious
bugger, too. You and Mabel are well met.

(*At first* O'DONNELL *reads his portions of the submission in*

mocking and exaggerated tones. He is unaware that O'NEILL *is
deadly serious. But as they proceed through the document –*
O'DONNELL *reading his sections,* O'NEILL *speaking his by heart
–* O'DONNELL's *good humour drains away and he ends up as
formal and as grave as* O'NEILL.)

(*Reads*) I, Hugh O'Neill, by the Queen of England, France
and Ireland her most gracious favour created Earl of Tyrone,
do with all true and humble penitency prostrate myself at her
royal feet – (O'DONNELL *drops on his knees*) – absolutely submit
myself to her mercy. (*Not reading*) Mercy, Queen, Mercy!

O'NEILL: Most sorrowfully imploring her gracious commiseration
and appealing only to her princely clemency, without
presuming to justify my unloyal proceedings against her
sacred majesty.

O'DONNELL: (*Reads*) May it please her majesty to mitigate her
just indignation against me for my unnatural rebellion which
deserves no forgiveness and for which I can make no
satisfaction, even with my life. (*Not reading*) Jesus, you are
one great fraud, O'Neill!

O'NEILL: I do most humbly beg her majesty to restore me to my
former living and dignity where as an obedient subject I vow
to continue hereafter loyal to her royal person, to her crown,
to her prerogatives, and to her English laws.

O'DONNELL: Her English – ?! Hey, steady on, man, steady – !

O'NEILL: I do renounce and abjure all foreign power whatever and
all kind of dependency upon any other potentate but Her
Majesty, the Queen of England, France and Ireland –

O'DONNELL: (*Reads*) And do vow to serve her faithfully against
any foreign power invading her kingdom; and especially do I
abjure and renounce all manner of dependency upon the King
of Spain and shall be ready with the uttermost of my ability to
serve Her Majesty against him or any of his forces or
confederates.

O'NEILL: I do resign all claim and title to any lands but such as shall
now be granted to me; and lastly I offer to the Queen and to
her magistrates here my full assistance in anything that may
tend to the advancement of her service and the peaceable
government of this kingdom.

O'DONNELL: (*Reads*) Particularly will I help in the abolishing of all barbarous Gaelic customs which are the seeds of all incivility.

O'NEILL: And for the clearing of all difficult passages and places –

O'DONNELL: (*Reads*) Which are the nurseries –

O'NEILL: Which are the nurseries of rebellion. And I will endeavour to erect habitations –

O'DONNELL: (*Reads*) Civil habitations.

O'NEILL: Civil habitations for myself and for the people of my country to preserve us against any force but the power of the state –

O'DONNELL: (*Reads*) By which power –

O'NEILL: By which power we must rest assured to be preserved as long as we continue in our loyal and faithful duties to Her Majesty –

O'DONNELL: (*Reads*) To her most clement –

O'NEILL: To her most clement, most gracious, most noble and most forgiving majesty.

O'DONNELL: (*Reads*) To whom I now most abjectly and most obediently offer my service and indeed . . . my life . . . (*Silence. Then* O'NEILL *moves away as if to distance himself from what he has just said.* O'DONNELL *is still on his knees.*) This is the end of it all, Hugh, isn't it? (*Pause.*) Jesus. (*He gets to his feet. Brightening*) All the same they say she's a peculiar woman, the Queen. Damn it, wouldn't it be a good one if she believed you – eh?

O'NEILL: She won't believe me.

O'DONNELL: But if she did! Damn it, I'd make a submission to her myself!

O'NEILL: Belief has nothing to do with it. As Mabel says, she'll use me if it suits her.

O'DONNELL: And your people?

O'NEILL: They're much more pure, 'my people'. Oh, no, they won't believe me either. But they'll pretend they believe me and then with ruthless Gaelic logic they'll crucify me for betraying them.

(HARRY *enters. He looks quickly first at* O'NEILL *and then at*

50

O'DONNELL – *they have not noticed his arrival. He then greets them with deliberate heartiness.*)

HARRY: It wouldn't be hard to surprise you two.

O'DONNELL: Harry! How are you, man?

HARRY: When did you get back?

O'DONNELL: Just arrived.

HARRY: We thought we had lost you – (*To* O'NEILL) didn't we?

O'DONNELL: I tried to surrender to Dowcra but he wouldn't take me.

O'NEILL: How was the journey?

HARRY: The journey was fine. We had a fine journey.

O'NEILL: And the O Cathains were expecting her?

HARRY: A big welcoming party. Everything quiet here?

O'NEILL: She was in good form when you left her?

HARRY: That's a great place they have there. (*To* O'DONNELL) Ethna O Cathain and your mother are cousins, aren't they?

O'DONNELL: Second cousins.

HARRY: Yes, she mentioned that. (*Rummaging in his bag*) And she sent you both some food: some oatmeal bread and milk and what's this – biscuits – strange-looking biscuits –

O'NEILL: They know exactly where I am?

HARRY: Of course they know; raisins, flour –

O'NEILL: And they'll send me word immediately?

HARRY: Yes. And she sent this specially to you, Hugh.

(*He hands over a bottle to* O'DONNELL.)

O'DONNELL: Is it whiskey?

HARRY: Ten year old.

O'DONNELL: Decent woman, Ethna. And thank God I don't put water in it.

HARRY: Anybody else hungry?

O'NEILL: No, thanks.

O'DONNELL: (*Drinking*) Good luck. Hugh?

O'NEILL: Not for me.

O'DONNELL: What's the news about Dungiven, Harry?

HARRY: (*Eating*) Let me see. Nothing very much. Archbishop Lombard's gone to Rome.

O'DONNELL: For good?

HARRY: They've invented some sort of job for him there.

O'DONNELL: You may be sure aul Peter'll always land on his feet.

HARRY: And Archbishop Oviedo's gone to England. The morning after Kinsale he headed straight for London to sweeten the authorities there – in case there'd be a backlash against the Catholics in England.

O'DONNELL: They don't miss a beat, those boys, do they? Beautiful stuff this. Sure you don't want some, Hugh?

HARRY: Leave some for the rest of us.

O'NEILL: They have their own physicians, the O Cathains, haven't they?

HARRY: Sean O Coinne. I met him there. Seemed very competent. What else is new? Oh, yes, Sir Garret Moore wants to get in touch with you – I imagine at Mountjoy's prompting. He wants to explore what areas of common interest might still exist between you and the crown. The pretext for getting you down to the Boyne is the first run of sea trout. If you were to go, I'm sure he'd have some civil servants there.

O'DONNELL: So they do want to talk to you, Hugh. Mabel was right.

HARRY: What else? . . . There's a rumour that Mountjoy himself may be in trouble because of some woman in England – Lady Penelope Rich? – is that the name? Anyhow if the scandal becomes public they say Mountjoy may be recalled. What else was there . . .? Sean na bPunta is still going calmly round the country with his brown leather bag, collecting your rents as if the place weren't in chaos! . . . Tadhg O Cianain is writing a book on the past ten years –

O'DONNELL: Another history! Jesus, if we had as many scones of bread as we have historians!

HARRY: It will be a very exact piece of work that Tadhg will produce . . . And portions of another book are being circulated and it seems the English government is paying a lot of attention to it. Written by an Englishman called Spenser who used to have a place down near the Ballyhouras mountains – wherever they are – I'm getting like you, Hugh – they're in County Cork, aren't they? – anyhow this Spenser was burned out in the troubles after the battle of the Yellow

Parrallel - 1st hear of Mabel

FORD – (*He suddenly breaks down but continues speaking without stopping.*) Oh, my God, Hugh, I don't know how to say it to you – I don't know how to tell you – we had only just arrived at O Cathain's place – Interupts politics...

O'DONNELL: Harry – ?

HARRY: And the journey *had* been fine – she was in wonderful form – we sang songs most of the way – I taught her 'Tabhair Dom Do Lamh', Ruadhaire Dall's song, because the O Cathains are relatives of his and she could show off before them and we laughed until we were sore at the way she pronounced the Irish words – and she taught me a Staffordshire ballad called 'Lord Brand, He was a Gentleman' and I tried to sing it in a Staffordshire accent – and she couldn't have been better looked after – they were all waiting for her – Ethna, the doctor O Coinne, two midwives, half-a-dozen servants. And everything seemed perfectly normal – everything *was* fine. She said if the baby was a boy she was going to call it Nicholas after her father and if it was a girl she was going to call it Joan after your mother – and when Ethna asked her were you thinking of going into exile she got very agitated and she said, 'Hugh?' She said, 'Hugh would never betray his people' – and just then, quite normally, quite naturally, she went into labour – and whatever happened – I still don't really know – whatever happened, something just wasn't right, Hugh. The baby lived for about an hour – it was a boy – but she never knew it had died – and shortly afterwards Ethna was sitting on a stool right beside her bed, closer than I am to you – and she was sleeping very peacefully – and then she gave a long sigh as if she were very tired and when Ethna put her hand on her cheek . . . It wasn't possible to get word to you – it all happened so quickly – herself and the baby within two hours – the doctor said something about poisoning of the blood – Oh, God, I'm so sorry for you – I'm so sorry for all of us. I loved her, too – you know that – from the very first day we met her – remember that day in May? – her twentieth birthday? – she was wearing a blue dress with a white lace collar and white lace cuffs . . . If you had seen her laid out

she looked like a girl of fourteen, she was just so beautiful
. . . God have mercy on her. God have mercy on all of us.
(*Long silence.*)

O'NEILL: (*Almost in a whisper*) Yes, I think I'll take some of
that whiskey now, Hugh. Just a thimbleful, if you please.
And no water. Oh, dear God . . .
(*Quick black.*)

SCENE 2

Exile

O'Neill's apartment in Rome many years later.
When the scene opens the only light on the stage is a candle on a
large desk. This is Lombard's desk; littered with papers; and in the
centre is a large book – the history. The room is scantily furnished –
a small table, some chairs, a stool, a couch.

O'NEILL *is now in his early sixties. His eyesight is beginning*
to trouble him – he carries a walking stick. And he drinks too
much. We first hear his raucous shouting off. When he enters we see
that he is slightly drunk. His temper is volatile and bitter and
dangerous. He is carrying a lighted taper.

O'NEILL: (*Off*) Anybody at home? Harry? Why are there no
damned lights out here? (*Now on*) Catriona? Your slightly
inebriated husband is back! I really shouldn't have had
that last bottle of – (*He bumps into a stool and knocks it*
over. As he straightens it) Forgive me. I do beg your
pardon. Perhaps you could assist me, signor. Am I in the
right building? You see, I'm a foreigner in your city, an
émigré from Ireland in fact – yes, yes, *Irlanda*. Ah! You've
been there? *Bella*, indeed; indeed *bellissima*; you are very
kind. What's that? Oh, yes, that is perfectly true –
everybody does love us. And I'll tell you why, my friend:
because we are a most attractive and a most loyal people.
Now, if you'd be so kind, I'm trying to make my way to
the Palazzo dei Penitenzieri which is between the Via della
Conciliazione and the Borgo Santo Spirito where I live
with –
(*He breaks off suddenly because, holding his taper up high, he*

54

*finds himself standing at the desk and looking down at the book.
He stares at it for a few seconds.*)

(*Very softly*) The right building indeed. Home. Everything is
in order . . . (*He takes a few steps away from the desk. Calls*)
Archbishop? Harry?

(*No answer. He returns to the book and turns it round so that he
can read it. He leans over the page, his face close to it, and
reads:*)

'In the name of God. Herewith I set my hand to chronicle the
life of Hugh O'Neill, Earl of Tyrone, son of Feardorcha, son
of Conn Bacagh, son of Conn Mor, noblest son of noble
lineage who was fostered and brought up by the high-born
nobles of his tribe, the O'Hagans and the O'Quinns, and
who continued to grow and increase in comeliness and
urbanity, tact and eloquence, wisdom and knowledge,
goodly size and noble deeds, so that his name and fame
spread throughout the five provinces of Ireland and
beyond – ' (*Suddenly, violently, angrily he swings away from
the desk. Bellows*) Where the hell is everybody? Catriona?
Your devoted earl is home! (*Listens. No sound.*) At vespers,
no doubt. Or in the arms of some sweaty Roman with a thick
neck and a bushy stomach. *contrast*

(*He goes to the small table and lights the candles there. Then he
empties the dregs from two empty bottles into a wine glass. As he
does these things:*)

Enormously popular in this city, my Countess. Of course she
is still attractive – indeed all the more attractive since she has
gone ever so slightly, almost judiciously, to seed; no doubt
an intuitive response to the Roman preference for over-
ripeness. Curious people, these Romans: they even find her
vulgar Scottish accent charming. Happily for them they
don't understand a word she . . .

(*With the glass in his hand he has drifted back to – cannot resist
the pull of – the open book. Again myopically he leans over it and
reads:*)

'And people reflected in their minds that when he would
reach manhood there would not be one like him of the Irish
to avenge their wrongs and punish the plunderings of his

race. For it was foretold by prophets and by predictors of
futurity that there would come one like him –
    A man, glorious, pure, faithful above all
    Who will cause mournful weeping in every territory.
    He will be a God-like prince
    And he will be king for the span of – '
(*He shuts the book in fury.*)
Damn you, Archbishop! But this is one battle I am not going
to lose! (*Wheeling away from the table, bellowing*) Where the
hell is everybody?! Catriona, you bitch, where are you?
Haaaa–reeee!
(*He turns round.* HARRY *is at his elbow. He is embarrassed.*)
Ah, there you are. Why do you keep hiding on me? Where
the hell is everybody?

HARRY: Catriona has gone out. She says –

O'NEILL: (*Furious again*) Out! Out! Tell me when the hell my
    accommodating wife is ever in! (*Softly*) Sorry.

HARRY: And the Archbishop is upstairs. You were to have spent
    the afternoon with him.

O'NEILL: Why would I have done that?

HARRY: He wanted confirmation of some details.

O'NEILL: What are you talking about?

HARRY: For his history.

O'NEILL: 'His history'! Damn his history. I haven't eaten all day,
    Harry. I suppose I ought to be hungry.

HARRY: Let me get you –

O'NEILL: No, I don't want food. What's happened here since
    morning?

HARRY: A reply from the King of Spain.

O'NEILL: Wonderful!

HARRY: Eventually. Thanking you for your last three letters –

O'NEILL: But –

HARRY: But reminding you again that England and Spain have
    signed a peace treaty. It's fragile but it's holding.

O'NEILL: The King of Spain has betrayed us, Harry.

HARRY: He believes that the interests of Ireland and Spain are
    best served by '*inacción*'.

O'NEILL: *Inacción.*

HARRY: And he urges you to remain in Rome for the time being.

O'NEILL: I have remained in Rome for the time being at his insistence for the past eight years!

HARRY: He says he values your Christian patience.

O'NEILL: (*Shouts*) He values my Christian – ! (*Softly*) I'm going to die in this damned town, Harry. You do know that, don't you? And be buried here, beside my son, in the church of San Pietro. (*Laughs.*) The drink makes God-like princes maudlin.

HARRY: Not a good day?

O'NEILL: Oh, wonderful! Animating! The usual feverish political activity and intellectual excitement. First I walked to the top of the Janiculum hill. Then I walked down again. Then I stood in line at the office of the Papal Secretary and picked up my paltry papal pension and bowed and said, 'Grazie. Grazie molto.' Then I stood in line at the office of the Spanish Embassy and picked up my paltry Spanish pension and bowed and said, 'Gracias, Muchas gracias'. And then I – (*He breaks off, points to the ceiling.*) The Archbishop?
(HARRY *nods yes.*)
(*Whispers*) Then I spent a most agreeable hour with Maria the Neapolitan.

HARRY: That's a new name.

O'NEILL: Yes. Wonderful girl, Maria. Steeped in Greek mythology and speaks half-a-dozen languages. Anyhow I left some of my money with her; Spanish money, of course. And when I was leaving, d'you know what she said to me, Harry? 'Grazie, signor. Grazie molto.'
(HARRY *laughs.*)
She did. And I believe she meant it. I'm an old man – I was flattered momentarily.

HARRY: And then you met Neachtain O Domhnaill and Christopher Plunkett.

O'NEILL: Have you been spying on me?

HARRY: They were here this morning looking for you.

O'NEILL: And we spent the afternoon together – as you can see.

HARRY: O Domhnaill was drunk when he was here.

O'NEILL: And once more we went over the master plan to raise an

57

still living dream

army and retake Ireland. Spain will provide the men, France will supply the artillery and the Pope will pay for the transportation. Naturally O'Neill of Tyrone will lead the liberating host. But because my eyesight is less than perfect, Plunkett will ride a few paces ahead of me. And because Plunkett's hearing is less than perfect, O Domhnaill will ride a few paces ahead of him. O Domhnaill's delirium tremens has got to be overlooked because he refuses to acknowledge it himself. Our estimate is that it may take the best part of a day to rout the English – perhaps two if they put up a fight. The date of embarkation – May 19: you see, the eighteenth is pension day. *illusion*

HARRY: What drinking house were you in?

O'NEILL: Pedro Blanco's. Full as usual. Plunkett insisted the customers were all Englishmen, disguised as Romans, spying on us. And so for security reasons our master plan has been codenamed – this was O Domhnaill's only inspiration – Operation Turf Mould . . . I can't stand it much longer, Harry. I think my mind is beginning to . . . Maybe I should eat something. *alcoholic*

HARRY: Good. I'll get you –

O'NEILL: Not now. Later. If you would be so kind –
    (*He holds out his glass for* HARRY *to fill.*)

HARRY: Sorry, Hugh. We're out of wine. There's no wine in the house.

O'NEILL: Why?

HARRY: (*Reluctantly*) The supplier turned me away this afternoon. I'm afraid we've run out of credit.

O'NEILL: Who is this supplier?

HARRY: His name is Carlo something. We've always dealt with him. His place is at the back of –

O'NEILL: And he refused you?

HARRY: We already owe him eight hundred ducats.

O'NEILL: He refused you?

HARRY: He's a decent man but he has six young children.

O'NEILL: (*Shouts*) Don't be so damned elusive, Harry. (*Softly*) Did this fellow refuse you?

HARRY: He refused me.

O'NEILL: And he knew who the wine was for?

HARRY: I'm sure he did.

O'NEILL: Did you tell him the wine was for Hugh O'Neill?

HARRY: I've been going to him ever since we –

O'NEILL: Did you specifically tell him the wine was for Hugh O'Neill?

HARRY: Yes, of course he knew the wine was for Hugh O'Neill and what he said was that Hugh O'Neill's credit was finished – no payment, no wine. And you might as well know, too, that we owe money to Catriona's tailor and to the baker and that the rent in this place is six months overdue. *debt*

O'NEILL: (*Icy*) You're shouting at me, Harry. *still loyal*

HARRY: Sorry. I can't stand it much longer either, Hugh.

O'NEILL: And perhaps this is as good a time as any to take a look at how you're squandering the money I entrust to you to manage my affairs, or perhaps more importantly *why* you're squandering that money. Because my suspicion is that this isn't just your customary ineptitude in money matters –

(HARRY *goes to the door*.)

HARRY: We'll talk tomorrow, Hugh.

O'NEILL: What I suspect is that the pride you once professed in being a servant of the O'Neill is long gone – and I suppose that's understandable: I can't be of much use to you any more, can I? *decline*

HARRY: You suspect everybody and – *pretends understanding*

O'NEILL: And because that pride is gone, what I suspect is that some perverse element in your nature isn't at all displeased to see Hugh O'Neill humiliated by this anonymous back-street wine-vendor. *Back stabbing*

HARRY: Hugh –

O'NEILL: But it does distress me to see you so soured that it actually pleases you to have the bailiffs fling O'Neill out on the street. What's gnawing at you, Harry? Some bitterness? Some deep disappointment? Some corroding sense of betrayal? *Back stabbing*

HARRY: Soured? You talk to me about being soured, about betrayal? (*Controls himself.*) Leave the door open for the Countess.

Back to heads [handwritten annotation]

O'NEILL: What was it I called you once, Harry? Was it borage? No, that was O'Donnell, may he rest in peace; loyal, faithful Hugh. No, you were . . . dill! The man with the comforting and soothing effect! And the interesting thing is that I chose Harry Hoveden to be my private secretary precisely because he wasn't a Gael. You see, I thought a Gael might be vulnerable to small, tribal pressures – to little domestic loyalties – an almost attractive human weakness when you come to think of it. So instead I chose one of the Old English because he would be above that kind of petty venality. So I chose Harry Hoveden because he claimed to admire Hugh O'Neill and everything Hugh O'Neill was attempting to do for his people and because when he left the Old English and joined us he protested such fealty and faithfulness not only to Hugh O'Neill but to the whole Gaelic nation.

dill [handwritten annotation, left margin]

nasty [handwritten annotation, left margin]

HARRY: If you weren't so drunk, Hugh –

(*He breaks off because* LOMBARD *enters.*)

O'NEILL: The fault, of course, is mine. I suppose that easy rejection of his old loyalties and the almost excessive display of loyalty to us ought to have alerted me. Certainly Mabel was never taken in by it. *untrue* [handwritten annotation]

HARRY: I'm sorry for you, Hugh. You have become a pitiable, bitter bastard.

O'NEILL: Don't you believe in loyalty any more, Harry? In keeping faith? In fealty?

(LOMBARD *assesses the situation instantly and accurately and in response he assumes a breezy, energetic manner which he sustains right through the scene. As he enters he holds up a bottle.*

Bad acting [handwritten annotation, left margin]

O'NEILL *immediately regrets his outburst but is unable to apologize and slumps sulkily in a chair.*)

LOMBARD: I've come at a bad moment, have I? No? Good. And look what I have here. You'd never guess what this is, Harry.

HARRY: A bottle.

LOMBARD: Brilliant. D'you see, Hugh?

O'NEILL: Yes.

LOMBARD: Arrived this very day. From home. But it's a very special bottle, Harry. Poitín. Waterford poitín. I was never much help to their spiritual welfare but they certainly don't neglect the state of my spirit! (*Laughs*.) Have you some glasses there? (*To* O'NEILL) Catriona says she'll be late, not to wait up for her. Something about a tailor and a dress fitting. (*To* HARRY) Good man. This, I assure you, is ambrosia.

HARRY: Not for me, Peter. But he needs some very badly.

(*As* HARRY *leaves* LOMBARD *calls after him.*)

LOMBARD: I'll leave this aside for you and if you feel like joining us later . . . And for the Earl himself, just a drop. It's pure nectar, Hugh. (*He takes a sip and relishes it.*) Tell me this: are the very special delights of this world foretastes of eternity or just lures to perdition? It's from my own parish; a very remote place called Affane, about ten miles from Dungarvan. And it has been made there for decades by an old man who claims he's one of Ormond's bastards. If he is, God bless bastards – God forgive me. (*Takes another sip.*) Exquisite, isn't it? Affane must be an annex of heaven – or Hades.

(O'NEILL *puts his untouched drink to the side.*)

O'NEILL: I'll try it later, Peter.

LOMBARD: Of course. Now. (*Going to his desk*) You're not too tired to help me check a few details, are you? Splendid. (*Sees the book has been closed.*) You know, Hugh, you were very naughty today.

O'NEILL: Was I?

LOMBARD: You and I were to have spent the afternoon on this.

O'NEILL: What's that?

LOMBARD: My history. (*Laughs.*) 'My history'! You would think I was Thucydides, wouldn't you? And if the truth were told, I'm so disorganized I'm barely able to get all this stuff into chronological order, not to talk of making sense of it. But if I'm to write about the life and times of Hugh O'Neill, the co-operation of the man himself would be a help, wouldn't it?

O'NEILL: Sorry, Peter.

LOMBARD: No harm done. Here we are – let me tell you the broad outline.

O'NEILL: I had a bad day.

: I know. Pension day. That's understandable.

: A stupid, drunken day with Plunkett and O Dohmnaill.

ARD: I saw them this morning. A sorry sight. They were two great men once.

O'NEILL: And I was cruel to Harry just now.

LOMBARD: I sensed something was amiss.

O'NEILL: I told him Mabel didn't trust him. That was a damned lie. Mabel loved Harry.

LOMBARD: I know she did. And Harry understands. We all understand. It's been a difficult time for you, Hugh. That's why this history is important – is vitally important. These last years have been especially frustrating. But what we must remember – what I must record and celebrate – is the *whole* life, from the very beginning right through those glorious years when aspiration and achievement came together and O'Neill was a household name right across Europe. Because they were glorious, Hugh. And they are a cause for celebration not only by us but by the generations that follow us. Now. (*Finds his outline.*) I think this is it – is it? Yes, it is.

O'NEILL: Mabel will be in the history, Peter?

LOMBARD: Mabel? What sort of a question is that? Of course Mabel will be in the history.

O'NEILL: Central to it, Peter.

LOMBARD: And so will your first wife, Brian MacFelim's daughter. And so will your second, the wonderful Siobhan. And so will Mabel. And so will our beautiful Catriona – she says not to wait up for her. They'll all be mentioned. What a strange question! (*Confidentially*) But I've got to confess a secret unease, Hugh. The fact that the great Hugh O'Neill had four wives – and there were rumours of a fifth years and years ago, weren't there? – long before you and I first met – but the fact that O'Neill had four, shall we say acknowledged, wives, do you think that may strike future readers as perhaps . . . a surfeit? I'm sure not. I'm sure I'm being too sensitive. Anyhow we can't deliberately suppress what we know did happen, can we? So. Back to my overall framework.

O'NEILL: This is my last battle, Peter.

LOMBARD: Battle? What battle?

O'NEILL: That [*book*].

LOMBARD: What are you talking about?

O'NEILL: That thing there.

LOMBARD: Your history?

O'NEILL: *Your* history. I'm an old man. I have no position, no
power, no money. No, I'm not whingeing – I'm not
pleading. But I'm telling you that I'm going to fight you on
that and I'm going to win.

LOMBARD: Fight – ? What in the name of God is the man talking
about?

O'NEILL: I don't trust you. I don't trust you to tell the truth.

LOMBARD: To tell the truth in – ? Do you really think I would – ?

O'NEILL: I think you are not trustworthy. And that [*book*] is all
that is left to me.

LOMBARD: You *are* serious! Hugh, for heaven's sake – !
(LOMBARD *bursts out laughing*.)

O'NEILL: Go ahead. Laugh. But I'm going to win this battle,
Peter.

LOMBARD: Hold on now – wait – wait – wait – wait. Just tell me
one thing. Is this book some sort of a malign scheme? Am I
doing something reprehensible?

O'NEILL: You are going to embalm me in – in – in a florid lie.

LOMBARD: Will I lie, Hugh?

O'NEILL: I need the truth, Peter. That's all that's left. The
schemer, the leader, the liar, the statesman, the lecher, the
patriot, the drunk, the soured, bitter émigré – put it *all* in,
Peter. Record the *whole* life – that's what you said yourself.

LOMBARD: Listen to me, Hugh –

O'NEILL: I'm asking you, man. Yes, damn it, I am pleading.
Don't embalm me in pieties.

LOMBARD: Let me tell you what I'm doing.

O'NEILL: You said Mabel will have her place. That place is
central to me.

LOMBARD: Will you listen to me?

O'NEILL: Can I trust you to make Mabel central?

LOMBARD: Let me explain what my outline is. May I? Please?
And if you object to it – or to any detail in it – I'll rewrite the

63

whole thing in any way you want. That is a solemn promise. Can I be fairer than that? Now. I start with your birth and your noble genealogy and I look briefly at those formative years when you were fostered with the O'Quinns and the O'Hagans and received your early education from the bards and the poets. I then move –

O'NEILL: England.

LOMBARD: What's that?

O'NEILL: I spent nine years in England with Leicester and Sidney.

LOMBARD: You did indeed. I have all that material here. We then look at the years when you consolidated your position as the pre-eminent Gaelic ruler in the country, and that leads on to those early intimations you must have had of an emerging nation state. And now we come to the first of the key events: that September when all the people of Ulster came together at the crowning stone at Tullyhogue outside Dungannon, and the golden slipper is thrown over your head and fastened to your foot, and the white staff is placed in your right hand, and the True Bell of St Patrick peals out across the land, and you are proclaimed . . . The O'Neill.

O'NEILL: That was a political ploy.

LOMBARD: It may have been that, too.

O'NEILL: The very next month I begged Elizabeth for pardon.

LOMBARD: But an occasion of enormous symbolic importance for your people – six hundred and thirty continuous years of O'Neill hegemony. Right, I then move on to that special relationship between yourself and Hugh O'Donnell; the patient forging of the links with Spain and Rome; the uniting of the whole of Ulster into one great dynasty that finally inspired all the Gaelic chieftains to come together under your leadership. And suddenly the nation state was becoming a reality. And talking of Hugh O'Donnell – (*He searches through a pile of papers.*) This will interest you. Yes, maybe this will put your mind at ease. Ludhaidh O'Cleary has written a life of Hugh and this is how he describes him. Listen to this. 'He was a dove in meekness

64

and gentleness and a lion in strength and force. He was a
sweet-sounding trumpet – '

O'NEILL: 'Sweet-sounding'!

LOMBARD: Listen! ' – with power of speech and eloquence, sense
and counsel, with a look of amiability in his face which
struck everyone at first sight.'
(O'NEILL *laughs*.)

O'NEILL: 'A dove in meekness'!

LOMBARD: But you'll have to admit it has a ring about it. Maybe
you and I remember a different Hugh. But maybe that's not
the point.

O'NEILL: What is the point? That's certainly a bloody lie.

LOMBARD: Not a lie, Hugh. Merely a convention. And I'll come
to the point later. Now, the second key event: the Nine
Years War between yourself and England, culminating in the
legendary battle of Kinsale and the crushing of the most
magnificent Gaelic army ever assembled.

O'NEILL: They routed us in less than an hour, Peter. Isn't that
the point of Kinsale?

LOMBARD: You lost a battle – that has to be said. But the telling
of it can still be a triumph.

O'NEILL: Kinsale was a disgrace. Mountjoy routed us. We ran
away like rats.

LOMBARD: And again that's not the point.

O'NEILL: You're not listening to *me* now. We disgraced ourselves
at Kinsale.

LOMBARD: And then I come to my third and final key point; and
I'm calling this section – I'm rather proud of the title – I've
named it 'The Flight of the Earls'. That has a ring to it, too,
hasn't it? That tragic but magnificent exodus of the Gaelic
aristocracy –

O'NEILL: Peter –

LOMBARD: When the leaders of the ancient civilization took boat
from Rathmullan that September evening and set sail for
Europe.

O'NEILL: As we pulled out from Rathmullan the McSwineys
stoned us from the shore!

LOMBARD: Then their journey across Europe when every

crowned head welcomed and fêted them. And then the final coming to rest. Here. In Rome.

O'NEILL: And the six years after Kinsale – before the Flight of the Earls – aren't they going to be recorded? When I lived like a criminal, skulking round the countryside – my countryside! – hiding from the English, from the Upstarts, from the Old English, but most assiduously hiding from my brother Gaels who couldn't wait to strip me of every blade of grass I ever owned. And then when I could endure that humiliation no longer, I ran away! If these were 'my people' then to hell with my people! The Flight of the Earls – you make it sound like a lap of honour. We ran away just as we ran away at Kinsale. We were going to look after our own skins! That's why we 'took boat' from Rathmullan! That's why the great O'Neill is here – at rest – here – in Rome. Because we ran away.

LOMBARD: That is my outline. I'll rewrite it in any way you want.

O'NEILL: That is the truth. That is what happened.

LOMBARD: How should it be rewritten?

O'NEILL: Those are the facts. There is no way you can make unpalatable facts palatable. And your point – just what is your point, Peter?

LOMBARD: I'm no historian but –

O'NEILL: Then don't write my history. Or maybe you could trust me to write it myself: one of the advantages of fading eyesight is that it gives the imagination the edge over reality.

LOMBARD: May I try to explain something to you, Hugh? May I tell you what my point is?

O'NEILL: I'm weary of all this.

LOMBARD: People want to know about the past. They have a genuine curiosity about it.

O'NEILL: Then tell them the whole truth.

LOMBARD: That's exactly what my point is. People think they just want to know the 'facts'; they think they believe in some sort of empirical truth, but what they really want is a story. And that's what this will be: the events of your life categorized and classified and then structured as you would structure any story. No, no, I'm not talking about falsifying,

66

about lying, for heaven's sake. I'm simply talkin[...] making a pattern. That's what I'm doing with all [...] offering a cohesion to that random catalogue of de[...] achievement and sheer accident that constitutes yo[...] And that cohesion will be a narrative that people wi[...] and be satisfied by. And that narrative will be as true and as objective as I can make it – with the help of the Holy Spirit. Would it be profane to suggest that that was the method the Four Evangelists used? – took the haphazard events in Christ's life and shaped them into a story, into four complementary stories. And those stories are true stories. And we believe them. We call them gospel, Hugh, don't we? (*He laughs suddenly and heartily.*) Would you look at that man! What are you so miserable about? Think of this [*book*] as an act of *pietas*. Ireland is reduced as it has never been reduced before – we are talking about a colonized people on the brink of extinction. This isn't the time for a critical assessment of your 'ploys' and your 'disgraces' and your 'betrayal' – that's the stuff of another history for another time. Now is the time for a hero. Now is the time for a heroic literature. So I am offering Gaelic Ireland two things. I'm offering them this narrative that has the elements of myth. And I'm offering them Hugh O'Neill as a national hero. A hero and the story of a hero. (*Pause.*) It's a very worldly nostrum for a clergyman to propose – isn't it? I suppose, if I were a holy man, not some kind of a half priest, half schemer, I suppose I would offer them God and prayer and suffering. But there are times when a hero can be as important to a people as a God. And isn't God – or so I excuse my perfidy – isn't God the perfect hero?

(*A very long silence.* LOMBARD *gathers up his papers and closes the book.* O'NEILL *assimilates what he has heard.*)

O'NEILL: How do you write about Harry?

LOMBARD: What is the 'truth' about Harry? Well, we know, for example, that his Old English family threw him out, that he was destitute and that when you offered him a job, any job, he grabbed at it. We know, for example, that he was once passionately loyal to the Queen but that, when he joined you,

67

e seemed to have no problem in betraying that loyalty. Or simply – very simply – we know for example that Harry Hoveden was a man who admired and loved you without reservation and who has dedicated his whole life to you. For all I know there may be other 'truths' about Harry.

O'NEILL: Which are you recording?

LOMBARD: I know which one history prefers. As I keep telling you, histories are stories, Hugh, and stories prefer faithful friends, don't they? And isn't that the absolute truth about Harry? – is Harry Hoveden not a most faithful friend? (*Another long silence.*)

O'NEILL: And Mabel?

LOMBARD: Yes?

O'NEILL: (*Shouts*) Don't play bloody games with me, Archbishop! You know damned well what I'm asking you!

LOMBARD: You're asking me how Mabel will be portrayed.

O'NEILL (*Softly*): Yes, I'm asking you how Mabel will be portrayed.

LOMBARD: I've tried to explain that at this time the country needs a – *nature of a hero*

O'NEILL: How–will–Mabel–be–portrayed?
(*Pause.*) *Feet of clay*

LOMBARD: The story of your life has a broad but very specific sweep, Hugh –

O'NEILL: Peter, just – !

LOMBARD: And all those ladies you chose as your wives – splendid and beautiful and loyal though they undoubtedly were – well, they didn't contribute significantly to – what was it Mabel herself used to call it? – to the overall thing – wasn't that it? I mean they didn't reroute the course of history, did they? So I have got to be as fair as I can to *all* those ladies without diminishing them, without inflating them into something they were not, without lying about them. I mean our Catriona, our beautiful Catriona, would be the last to claim some historical eminence, wouldn't she? But they all did have their own scales; and they recognized what those dimensions were; and in fairness to them we should acknowledge those dimensions accurately.

use hist to make nture

O'NEILL: So Mabel . . . ?

LOMBARD: (*Pretended irritation*) You're incorrigible, Hugh
O'Neill! You know that, don't you? You never give up. All
I've got down on paper is a general outline and a couple of
opening pages and the man keeps badgering me about minor
details!

O'NEILL: So Mabel . . . ?

LOMBARD: Let me ask you a question. In the big canvas of
national events – in your exchanges with popes and kings and
queens – is that where Mabel herself thought her value and
her importance resided? Is that how she saw herself ? But she
had her own value, her own importance. And at some future
time and in a mode we can't imagine now I have no doubt
that story will be told fully and sympathetically. It will be a
domestic story, Hugh; a love story; and a very beautiful love
story it will be. But in the overall thing, Hugh . . . How
many heroes can one history accommodate? And how will I
emerge myself for Heaven's sake? At best a character in a
subplot. And isn't that adequate for minor people like us?
Now, Hugh, tell me, how do you want to rewrite my outline?

O'NEILL: The overall thing – yes, that was her expression.

LOMBARD: I made you a solemn promise. I'll rewrite it in any way
you want. What changes do you want me to make?
(*Pause.*)
Not necessarily anything major. (*Pause.*) Even small
adjustments. (*Pause.*) Just say the word.
(*Pause.*)
Now I'm badgering you – amn't I? Forgive me. And if any
idea or suggestion does occur to you over the next weeks or
months, sure I'll be here, won't I? Neither of us is going
anywhere – unless Plunkett and O Domhnaill recruit us for
their next expedition. Now. It's time for a drink. We've
earned it. My poor mouth's dry from blathering. Affane –
where are you?

O'NEILL: A lure to perdition – is that what you called it?

LOMBARD: A foretaste of immortality. It really is wonderful. Easy
– easy – don't gulp it down. Sip it slowly. Savour it.
(HARRY *enters, carrying a bottle.*)

Death images

Ah, Harry! We're just about to kill this bottle of poitín.
But, as the man says, it's not going to die without the priest.
Will somebody please hit me every time I make one of those
hoary clerical jokes? What's that you have?

HARRY: A bottle of wine.

LOMBARD: Where did that come from?

HARRY: I got it ten minutes ago.

O'NEILL: I thought we had no money?

HARRY: It's only cheap chianti.

O'NEILL: Where did the money come from?

loyal

HARRY: I had an old pair of shoes I didn't want. The porter had
some bottles to spare. Who wants a glass?

LOMBARD: Do you know what you are, Harry? A loyal and
faithful man. Now that is a truth!
(LOMBARD *pauses beside* HUGH *as he goes to the desk*.)
(*Privately*) Trust it, Hugh. Trust it. (*Aloud*) To all of us.
May we live for ever – in one form or another. And now I'm

Climax

going to give the first public recital of *The History of Hugh
O'Neill*. In the name of God – I know the opening by heart!
(*When* O'NEILL *speaks he speaks almost in a whisper in
counterpoint to* LOMBARD's *public recitation. His English accent
gradually fades until at the end his accent is pure Tyrone*.)
In the name of God. Herewith I set my hand to chronicle the
life of Hugh O'Neill –

O'NEILL: By the Queen of England, France and Ireland her most
gracious favour created Earl of Tyrone –

LOMBARD: Son of Feardorcha, son of Conn Bacagh, son of Conn
Mor, noblest son of noble lineage, who was fostered and
brought up by the high-born nobles of his tribe –

Letter to Queen

O'NEILL: I do with all true and humble penitency prostrate
myself at your feet and absolutely submit myself to your
mercy, most sorrowfully imploring your commiseration and
appealing only to your clemency – *Contrast - Lomb*

LOMBARD: He continued to grow and increase in comeliness and
urbanity, tact and eloquence, wisdom and knowledge,
goodly size and noble deeds so that his name and fame spread
throughout the five provinces of Ireland and beyond –

O'NEILL: May it please you to mitigate your just indignation

70

cleaning up play

against me for my betrayal of you which deserves no
forgiveness and for which I can make no satisfaction, even
with my life –

LOMBARD: And people reflected in their minds that when he
would reach manhood there would not be one like him of the
Irish to avenge their wrongs and punish the plunderings of
his race –

O'NEILL: Mabel, I am sorry . . . please forgive me, Mabel . . .

LOMBARD: For it was foretold by prophets and by predictors of
futurity that there would come one like him –

denhal A man, glorious, pure, faithful above all
Who will cause mournful weeping in every territory.
He will be a God-like prince
And he will be king for the span of his life.

(O'NEILL *is now crying. Bring down the lights slowly.*)

contrast

Drink
hist unclear.